W9-AVQ-492

Presented To

Melo

From

Wanda

Date

Happy Easter 2020

MARIE CHAPIAN has been teaching and writing inspirational books to empower Christians in their walk with God for over 20 years with more than 30 books translated into 15 languages, including Chinese and Arabic. Her Christian writings have earned the Gold Medallion and the Cornerstone Book of the Year awards, among others. Her books include *Telling Yourself the Truth*, *A HEART FOR GOD* devotional series, and *Free to Be Thin*. She holds a doctorate in counseling and a Master of Fine Arts degree in creative writing, is heard and seen on radio and TV, and travels widely as a conference speaker.

Visit Marie at *www.mariechapian.com*.

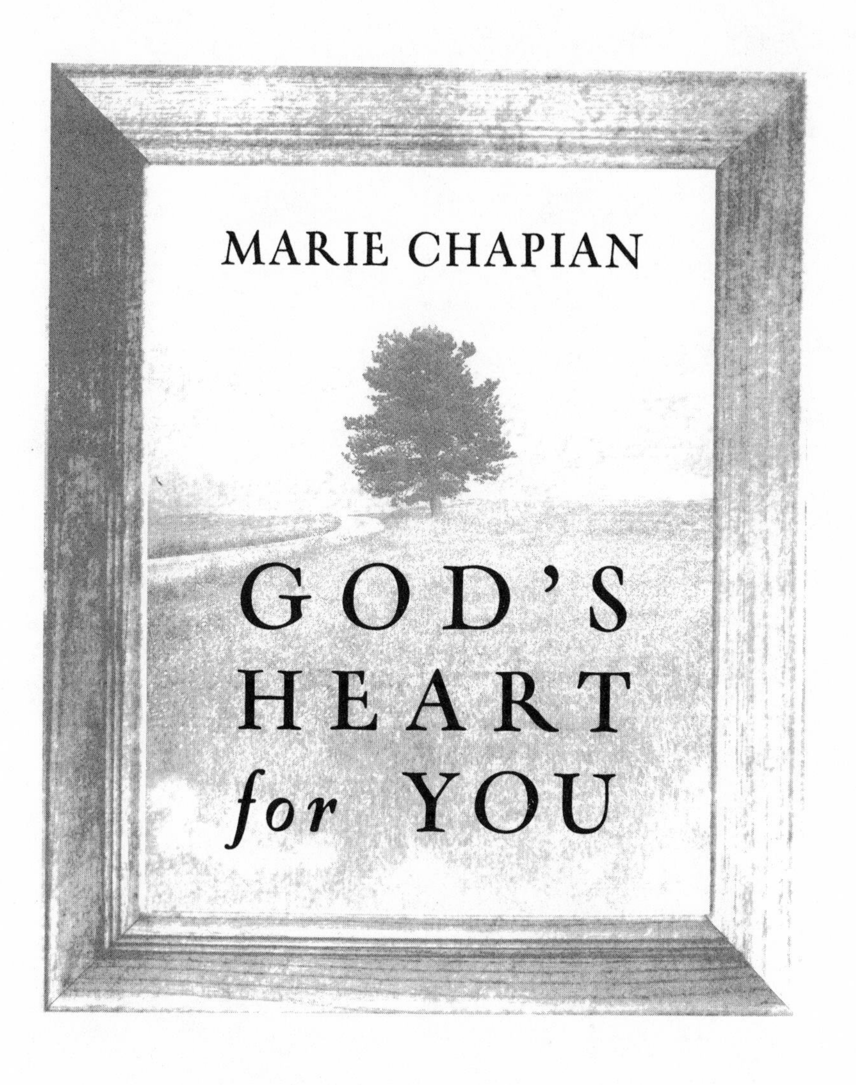

MARIE CHAPIAN

GOD'S HEART *for* YOU

BETHANY HOUSE
Minneapolis, Minnesota

God's Heart for You
Copyright © 2005
Marie Chapian

Cover design by Jennifer Parker

Published by Bethany House Publishers
11400 Hampshire Avenue South
Bloomington, Minnesota 55438

Bethany House Publishers is a division of
Baker Publishing Group, Grand Rapids, Michigan.

Printed in the United States of America

Library of Congress Cataloging-in-Publication Data

Chapian, Marie.
God's heart for you : daily promises of God's faithfulness in his own words / Marie Chapian.
p. cm.
Summary: "Scriptural meditations that touch the soul as readers listen to the Word in a fresh, personal way"—Provided by publisher.
ISBN 0-7642-0139-5
1. Bible—Meditations. I. Title.
BS491.5.C32 2005
242'.5—dc22 2005020517

Contents

Introduction

The Word of God is heaven flooding us with the magnificence of the Lord's perfect ways. The Lord continually calls to us, drawing us to himself, with His never-ending, omnipresent song of love. The Word of God lives, breathes, and is powerfully present at all times to lift us to a higher level in our faith and experience. *"'My sheep hear My voice, and I know them, and they follow Me'"* (John 10:27 NKJV).

This book is not mine by any means. I merely write down what I hear Him tell me through His Word. It began in 1987, when I presented to Bethany House the first book of my HEART FOR GOD devotional series, where the Lord did all the speaking. They liked what they read, and five books later almost a million souls have experienced the Lord's voice through the pages of those little books.

God's Heart for You is a culmination of the voice of God that spoke through those pages. It is with the same heartbeat and passion that we pursue a deeper intimacy with the King of Kings in these pages. While immersing myself in the expression of His heart, working on this book, I would become so overwhelmed with the magnitude of His longing for us to know Him and His great love that I would dissolve in a fit of weeping. Often I could barely hold the pen. I could only cling to my Bible, listen, and sob. At other times as I worked, I would find myself laughing. Sometimes I'd sigh, smile, gasp, even dance, at His Word. One thing is for certain: When the Holy Spirit ignites the Word of God in our hearts, we can't remain passive. No, we must act! Focused on God's words of compassion and mercy, we can feel at once the unfathomable wealth of His tender care and high calling for us. With so many amazing promises ours, we are able to hear and follow His voice of guidance, instruction, and correction. (Discipline comes easier to us when from the gentle hand of love.)

The living presence of the Lord will always change us and bring us to our knees and to our truest selves. How miraculous and unfathomable is the intimacy the Father offers us through His Word.

It is my desire that when you read His words in this book, you'll develop a deeper hunger for prayer and intimacy with Jesus Christ, who *is* the Word (John 1:1). My most humble hope is that His voice will supersede the inadequate human vocabulary to speak directly into your heart. Before you open this book to read, please ask the Lord to speak to you directly for your specific need of the hour. Open your heart for His Spirit to sear with His love and power. He will answer. Take time to absorb what He wants to tell you. And please do look up the Scripture verses at the end of each devotional reading. Each verse has been lovingly prayed over to be an arrow into your soul.

I pray *God's Heart for You* touches, encourages, and ignites a more profound passion for the living presence of our Savior in your life. I pray His heart fuses into yours and that you experience Him new and fresh each time you pick up this book to hear from Him.

Lost in His Heart,

Marie

When I Speak to You

The voice of the LORD is powerful;
the voice of the LORD is full of majesty.

Psalm 29:4 KJV

I speak by My Spirit.
    You hear with the ears of spirit.
Hear Me.

All things happen in their appropriate time.
    There is a time for crying,
a time for laughing.
    There is a time for sorrow,
and a time to be carefree.
    There is time for plenty,
and a time for lack.
    All your times
are in My hands.
    Don't fret over the thorns
in your side.

Be glad
that the power within you
is greater than the struggle
around you.
I will cause
the voice of My authority
to be heard,
the majesty of My voice and the strength
of My arm will be known—
I am speaking to you now.
My voice carves flames of fire
in the breasts of your enemies.
My voice shakes the wilderness
like a shirt flapping in the wind,
putting an end to terror.
I will cause My power to multiply
on the earth as I strip away
the evil done My own. Listen.
I am instilling My thoughts in you.
I am climbing
the pinnacles
of the crucial hour

alongside you and within you.
Listen.
Don't miss this.

Genesis 3:8; John 10:27; Ezekiel 43:2; Isaiah 30:30;
Revelation 1:15; Romans 8:11; Joel 2:30–32

The Gift of Wholeness

But Jesus turned around, and when He saw her He said,
"Be of good cheer, daughter;
your faith has made you well."
And the woman was made well from that hour.

MATTHEW 9:22 NKJV

You were not created in bits and pieces,
you were created as a whole person.
I have created you to come to Me
in wholeness, not in parts.
When you come to Me for healing,
I do not see a part of you. I see
all of you. All of you cries out to Me.
Your faith touches the whole of you.
Your faith surges through you like a comet
dividing the winds of illness.
Your complete self responds, for you are not
a partial person, you are whole, and
I heal all of you.

I clean and heal your mind
so obsessed with fears and worries.
I heal the hurts and wounds
you've suffered in the past. I heal you wholly.
I forgive the devastating choices you've made,
the times of willingly sinning against yourself
and your body
and Me.
I give you peace to saturate
your emotions that easily tatter
by the cares of life.
I give you health complete.
I heal your body,
soul, and spirit,
for it is My will that your entire person
praise My Name.
I give you *more* than enough, for there is more
to you than you bring to Me.
Your body is as precious
to Me as your soul. I redeem
and heal, not partially,
but wholly. You are not a partial person.
You are whole. You are wholly saved, not
partially. Delight your whole self in Me,

body, soul, and spirit; not partially,
but wholly. Rest in your healing,
in the wholeness of your life in Me.

Colossians 2:10; Philippians 4:13; 1 Corinthians 15:49; 2 Corinthians 3:5; Proverbs 17:14; 1 Timothy 6:20; Isaiah 55:7; Philippians 2:5; Romans 8:11

Everything I Tell You Is True

It is impossible for God ever to prove false or deceive us.

Hebrews 6:18 AMP

I want you to know Who I am . . .

I want you to rise above
    circumstances around you.
Be anchored
    in knowing there are two things
since before creation that
    cannot change:
I cannot lie when I make a promise,
and I cannot lie
    when I make an oath.
You have fled to Me for strength
    and courage, and now I tell you,
hold fast and know the hope appointed you.
    Blessing, I will certainly bless you;

multiplying, I will multiply you.
My promise and purpose are unchangeable.
My plans for you are sealed with My divine
and perfect oath.
Come to Me inside the veil. Enter behind
the curtain, the Most Holy Place in heaven,
with My promise.
This place is the steadfast anchor for your soul,
so it won't slip or shatter
under any human foot. It reaches to the
very immutability of My Presence.
I tell you,
the joy of heaven is yours,
and I do not lie.
I want you to drink from the river
of My delights;
I want you to eat the fruit
of revelation in My Word.
Oh, take what I have for you!
Treasure My promises.
Everything I have is yours!

Psalm 31:19–21; 36:7–9; 119:105; Genesis 22:16–17;
Leviticus 16:2; Jeremiah 29:11; Luke 15:31

Become Familiar With My Voice

And I saw the glory of the God of Israel
coming from the east.
His voice was like the roar of rushing
waters, and the land was radiant
with his glory.

EZEKIEL 43:2 NIV

Can you describe My voice?
Listen for Me,
wait upon Me,
and experience the rush of many waters
over your soul
as the King of Glory comes in!
I am the voice
within the blinding white cloud,
within the thundering storm,
the voice that is heard after
the earthquake
and the consuming fire,
still and small.

My voice is great and covers the earth,
and it is hushed and gentle,
    both imperceptible to the non-spiritual ear.
I am the voice walking in the garden
    of your mind.

I stand at the front gate of your life,
    calling. Won't you welcome Me?
Come, embrace Me.
    I have wondrous things to tell you,
wondrous places to take you.
Hear Me.
Come to Me.
Open to Me.

Psalm 24:7; Matthew 17:5; 1 Kings 19:12; Genesis 3:8; Revelation 3:20

Take Your Place

You have given me the heritage
of those who fear your name.

Psalm 61:5b NIV

Now is the time
    for you to come up higher.
Now is the time
    to rise up and meet Me
in My garden of prayer.
    You are not a paper boat
afloat in a pond relying on a fickle
current and luck.
    You were born to know
    the glory of God!
You were born to dance on mountaintops
    and ride the chariots of success!
No longer will you mope and grovel,
allowing the world around you
    to dictate your level of faith.

You will take your place in My kingdom
and receive from Me.
You were born to be successful.
Take the present.
Live the present.
Love the present.
Take your place.

Psalm 34:1–3; Philippians 3:7, 14; Colossians 2:10; John 10:10; Isaiah 52:7; Matthew 6:9–13

The Gift of Security

Now to Him who is able to keep
you from stumbling,
and to present you faultless
before the presence of His glory
with exceeding joy. . . .

JUDE 1:24 NKJV

You ask why I permit evil
to exist,
why I allow My godly ones to suffer.
I tell you,
wherever evil is found,
it bears within itself
the seeds of its own destruction.
Evil will destroy itself.
Only in My righteousness is there power
to withstand and persevere;
only in My holiness can you withstand
the darts of evil.
Lean your entire human personality on Me,
for apart from Me you can do nothing.

Wrap My words around your heart,
tie them around your neck as a golden leash,
and when you go about your life,
My words will guide you. When you sleep,
My words will watch over you
to make sweet your dreams and keep you safe
from harm.
The sun will not scorch you by day,
nor will the moon obscure you by night.
I am the shade at your right hand. I watch
your coming and your going
now and forever.
Through My Son Jesus, you have eternal life,
and you have more than enough power
for this life
by the same spirit that raised Him from the dead.
Human understanding cannot
begin to understand this. I ask you
to give Me your human understanding
that I might set fire to it—
create sizzling, crackling flames of truth
within you.
You see, dear one,
you are secure,

not so much because you understand,
but because
I say so.

Psalm 118:5; Psalm 37:9; Psalm 34:21; Proverbs 14:19; Matthew 12:35; John 6:63; James 1:21; Proverbs 2:6–7; John 3:14–15; Romans 8:11; Psalm 121:5–8; Proverbs 6:20–21; Proverbs 2:2; Isaiah 40:8

The Hungry Heart

As the deer pants for the water brooks,
So pants my soul for You, O God.
My soul thirsts for God,
for the living God.

PSALM 42:1-2A NKJV

When you hunger for Me,
even the most bitter tastes in your mouth
will turn sweet.
When you love and hunger for Me,
you gain a deeper knowledge of the sacrifice
I made for you on the cross;
you envision more clearly, moment by moment,
the importance of your utter abandonment to Me.
Do you see how beautiful you are to Me?
Can you grasp that your new life is real,
lasting, and the genuine essence
of God Almighty
within you?
I know you. I know you when you sit down
and when you stand up. I can hear you

when you speak.
I understand your thoughts.
I am acquainted with your ways.
There are your ways,
and there are My ways.
There are your thoughts,
and there are My thoughts.
There is My Word,
and there are your words.
Give it all to Me.

I am everything to you.
I hold and maintain
what concerns you.
I am ever at your right hand.
Don't be moved by the interferences
and intrusions surrounding you.
Let your heart thirst and hunger for Me,
because only My presence can saturate and fill you
with joy and pleasure to thrive forever.
Be consumed by My love and
always ask for more.

Psalm 38:10; 139:1–5

LORD, TO BE ONE WITH YOU

But God, who is rich in mercy, because of His great love with which He loved us, even when we were dead in trespasses, made us alive together with Christ (by grace you have been saved), and raised us up together, and made us sit together in the heavenly places in Christ Jesus.

EPHESIANS 2:4 NKJV

Lord, I want Your Word alive in me,
so much so that I am no longer
ruled by the many problems
that surround me.
I want Your Word to drench my spirit.
I want to be filled with You
so I'm dominated by Your personality.
I want Your thoughts to permeate mine.
I long for You
and for Your peace
that passes my meager understanding.
I know You reward those

who diligently seek after You.
Can I be one with You?

Of course!
Oh beloved, the secret of the sweet,
satisfying friendship with Me
is yours!
When you live by My Holy Spirit,
I am always near and with you.
To be one with Me,
to walk one single path with Me,
is to fulfill your calling
and the highest aspiration
of a human being. I love you.
Come on up!

Hebrews 10:23; Galatians 5:25; Jeremiah 29:13; Psalm 25:14

Lord, I've Got Family Problems

Cause me to know the way in which I should walk,
for I lift up my soul to You.

Psalm 143:8 NKJV

Lord, I can't get along
with my family.
Is a harmonious home
too much to ask?

If you turn to Me,
listen to My instruction
and correction
through My Word,
you will discover the way of the family
and you'll see how I can transform
and heal the tattered
and seam-strained home.
Your loved ones need to see Me in you.

Your enemies are not flesh and blood.
Take a stand against your enemies
and stop being robbed
of My will for a beautiful Spirit-led home,
and declare daily, "As for me
and my house, we will serve the Lord!"
There is too much of you
in the way. I want to release you
from the manacles of bitterness
and discontent. I know your longing
for respect and understanding;
yes, I do. Can you give to those you love
what you most need yourself?
Can you be more tenderhearted,
compassionate, forgiving, just as I am
toward you? Godly families are formed
of My Spirit and by selfless work
on your part. Lose your mind and
take the mind of My Spirit,
and let the miracles begin.

Proverbs 10:17; 11:29; Ephesians 4:31–32; Matthew 7:7;
Zechariah 13:9; Acts 1:8

LISTEN TO MY VOICE

The sheep that are My own hear and are listening to My voice, and I know them and they follow Me.

JOHN 10:27 AMP

I speak to you day and night.
I love to talk to you,
I love to teach you, help you,
guide you every minute you breathe.
Every hair on your head
has a number. I know you. I know your going out
and your coming in,
I am your Lord,
and without Me you can do nothing.
I am speaking to you right now.
I am the still, small voice
quietly entering your heart
and your thoughts right now.
You are unique in My kingdom
and cherished by Me, and it is sweet
to speak to you this way. You are

absorbing My word
and My intensity of life as we speak.
Listen for Me early. When you awaken
in the morning, open your eyes and your ears
at the same time. As the new day coaxes you awake,
allow Me to kiss your thoughts with My words.
Allow My voice to embrace your mind with Mine.
Listen: Because you are Mine,
I gave you eternal life and your name
is forever engraved on the palm of My hand.
Nothing can snatch you away from Me
or take My love from you.
Listen: The Father and I are One,
as you and I are one. I am your Good Shepherd.
Yours. I am yours. I know you. *You are My own.*
And it is wonderful, My own, that you
recognize My voice, love Me, and hear Me.
Listen: I want you to continue to hear
My voice at all times. I want to be able
to speak to you and know you are listening.
I open the doors of My heavenly kingdom
for you to enter to hear, see, and learn
of My wonders.
Listen: I will bring you to a high place
where you will sit with Me. You will understand

excellence, virtue, and all that is worthy of praise. You will sing with angels and behold great and wonderful things.

Listen: I want My words to remain fixed and solid in you where they will thrive and bubble up with more revelation and knowledge into My heart and My mind.

And then, dear one,
as My own personal treasure,
created to bring delight to Me
and to all that is Mine,
you can ask Me whatever you will,
and it shall be done for you.

Just listen.

John 10:28–29; Philippians 4:8; 1 Corinthians 6:17; Ephesians 2:6; John 15:7; Mark 11:24

POWER ENCOUNTER

Go your way, eat the fat, drink the sweet, and send portions to him for whom nothing is prepared; for this day is holy to our Lord; and be not grieved and depressed, for the joy of the Lord is your strength and stronghold.

NEHEMIAH 8:10 AMP

You are favored by Me
because you have chosen
to live in My heart,
passionate and intimate
in the fire of My life.
You've entered the crucible of My love,
where I have captured every part
of your being. This intense
power encounter leads you to the blazing
flames of My love
that purify and consume.
I can speak to you
and you hear Me.

Where can you go from My Spirit?

If you ascend into My heaven,
I am there.
If you make your bed in Sheol,
the place of the dead,
I am there.
If you take the wings of the morning
and dwell in the uttermost parts of the sea,
even there My hand shall find yours
and I will pull you into Me.

If you say, "Surely the darkness shall cover me,
and the night shall be the only light about me,"
I am there, for to Me the night shines as day.

Before you took shape, I knew you. I wove you together in your mother's womb.

You were embroidered in the womb
like a tapestry, and the days of your life
were written in My book.

I give you My power to walk after the dictates of the Spirit
to fulfill My purposes.

Speak My language of victory.
I am your friend, your closest friend,
and all things in your life—

indeed all things—are working together, fitted into a plan,
wonderful and beautiful.
Meet Me on My terms, not yours.

John 15:11; Psalm 139:7–18; Romans 8:28

Lord, Why Can't I Be Happy?

Why are you cast down,
O my soul?
And why are you disquieted
within me?

Psalm 42:5 NKJV

Lord, why can't I
be happy?
It's as though a pretty little
candy cart is parked on my doorstep
and I keep throwing rocks at it.
Sometimes I think if pain were
handed out in big, free gift bundles,
I'd be the first in line.
Of course, I'd bitterly complain
and blame somebody else
for my troubles.
What's wrong with me?

I see you cringe and fumble
at the brink of blessing.
The prospect of a happy heart
frightens you.
At the moment of contentment
you crumble and withdraw.
You pray,
but you don't wait
for Me to answer.
You seek Me,
but by a wrong name.

My thoughts toward you are for good,
and not for evil.
My children who have given their lives
to Me
rise up victorious
over the enemies of the soul.
You, however, will not
rise up, for you have diffused
your soul in sand and
starved your spirit. You don't know Me.
I tell you, stop looking for the living
among the dead and come wholly to Me.

I give you all grace and
every favor and blessing.
I remove the frown
from your dear face.
I have created you
for a life of overcoming joy!
You are Mine, a precious treasure;
put down the rocks.

Isaiah 50:2–3; 2 Timothy 1:7; Jeremiah 29:11; 1 John 5:4; 2 Corinthians 9:8; Isaiah 43:1

When Your Temper Gets the Best of You

Cease from anger and forsake wrath;
fret not yourself; it tends only to evil-doing.
Psalm 37:8 AMP

I am the author of your emotions,
but anger keeps you from the sweet fulfillment
you crave in life.
I love your emotions, and I give you the right
to experience the emotion of anger. Yet do not sin,
do not let your fury or exasperation *continue.*

By allowing anger and bitterness
to remain in your heart, you invite
the enemy to influence
your reasoning as well as the choices
you make. Your mind
becomes stained, soiled,
damaged.
I tell you, give no opportunity to the devil.

The unruly temper produces polluted language
and worthless talk. I have called you
a child of light, which means
you live in and reflect *My* light. You are called
to walk as a child of light and lead a life
of holy wisdom. I want you
to refrain from all appearance of evil.
I want you to walk in goodness, trustworthy,
and content. There are no godly excuses
for an uncontrolled temper.

Do not delude or deceive yourself with vain
rationalizations
and useless arguments for sin. A volatile temper
destroys and tears down. It opens the door
for destruction
and failure.
Garrison and fill your mind with things that are
true, honest, right,
pure, beautiful, and respected. Above all else,
guard your heart
and your affections, for they influence
everything in your life.

Take a strong stand against anger
and ill temper, dear one.
Surrender.

James 1:20; Ephesians 4:26–27; Philippians 4:8; Proverbs 4:23

The Meaning of Mercy

Love covers over a multitude of sins.

1 Peter 4:8b NIV

Think of yourself
as a planter.
Think of yourself
as one who plants goodness,
that is, uprightness
and right-standing with Me.
When you are planted in Me,
you will reap a harvest of mercy
and loving-kindness. Blessed and
cherished are My merciful ones,
for they reap mercy. They walk in mercy
and are led with thoughts of mercy.
Mercy is wisdom and power, for I am
compassionate and gracious. It is time
to break up your uncultivated ground,
no longer an alien in your own land.

Stand upon My holy hill
    with clean hands, for if you would be
held in high regard in heavenly matters,
    you will carry the banner of mercy,
you will open your arms to extend forgiveness.
    Mercy and justice are among the affairs
of heaven. Your Lord and Savior
        never gossips,
        never lies, never breaks a promise,
        never acts or speaks unjustly.
I defend My own. What can harm you
    if you prove zealous for what is good?
Do not waste your emotions
    defending yourself or
seeking mercy from the wrong sources.
    Think of all you do as a fertile field
where you plant your good seeds.
    Let the mercy rain down.

Hosea 10:12; Matthew 5:7; Exodus 34:6; 1 Peter 3:13; James 4:10; Romans 9:23; Ezekiel 36:27; Matthew 18:33; Ephesians 4:32; James 2:13

THE GIFT OF RESPONSIBILITY

Do not be wise in your own eyes;
Fear the LORD and depart from evil.
It will be health to your flesh,
And strength to your bones.

PROVERBS 3:7–8 NKJV

You are not responsible for the body
you came to the earth with,
but you are fully in charge
of the one you bring to Me now.
How much has your body been influenced by
the pressures of your world, your
culture, your own lusts? I did not send My Son
to suffer for you on the cross
for your soul only. I have redeemed you,
spirit, soul, and body.
I want you to see My Spirit
engulfing your entire being.
If your body functions with limitations,

I love even that which does not function wholly,
because I love *you* wholly.
I do not give you partial redemption,
saving just some parts of you,
I save all of you so your body, soul, and spirit
will be filled with Me.
Open to Me, to My tender and perfect love for you
in your disabilities as well as
in your abilities. My love for you is perfect
in your health and in your lack of health.

Only your mind can cripple you.
Oh! My dearest, I am ever present in your pain.
I lift you up from the grip of fear
and bitter resignation. Come into My holy place
and rest with Me. Mold yourself into Me,
be responsible for faith that unleashes relief,
exquisite joy,
and inner health that no human power
can duplicate.

Proverbs 19:16; 12:24; 1 Peter 1:13–15, 5:8; Isaiah 53:5;
1 Corinthians 6:19; 1 Thessalonians 5:23; Matthew 22:37;
Psalm 107:20; Matthew 11:29

The Gift of More

Yet in all these things we are more than conquerors.

Romans 8:37 NKJV

To increase in Me,
you must decrease.
Do not settle for less from yourself
than learning to turn the other cheek
and to walk the second mile.
Do not accept giving only what is convenient.
Do not permit yourself to stand still
in a muddy spray of
ill temper and self-righteousness.
I know you.
And if I know you and love you,
and if I am for you,
who can be against you?
A conqueror is far more than one who endures
with slippery eyes and bitter heart.

A conqueror accepts the blow to the right cheek
and is glad for the opportunity
to turn the left cheek,
which I alone can see.
Begin to think:
MORE.

Romans 8:31

THE BIG IN THE SMALL

The wise in heart will be called discerning,
And sweetness of speech increases persuasiveness.

PROVERBS 16:21 NASB

Nothing is too small
 for Me.
I am in the grand events
 and in the very modest.
There is not a sigh too hushed
 that I cannot find it,
not a cell or microbe too infinitesimal
 for My touch to bring forth life.
Don't overlook the minute,
 the tiny, the seemingly insignificant.
 Listen for My delicate whisper,
the sound no thundering tempest
 can silence. Hear Me in the quiet
of the midnight hour, in the coo of early dawn.
 Hear Me. See Me.

I open your blind eye
    to see into the realm
of My Spirit,
    where you will find Me
in the blast of the trumpet
    and in the shadows
        of silence.

Psalm 131:1; Numbers 7:89; Psalm 68:33; Ezekiel 43:2; Isaiah 30:21; 1 Kings 19:12; Revelation 1:10; Ecclesiastes 3:7

Safe

My soul takes refuge and finds shelter and confidence in You; yes, in the shadow of Your wings will I take refuge.

Psalm 57:1 AMP

Have I forsaken you?
    Never!
Pause for a moment,
    and open the eyes of your spirit.
Who is the source of warmth and safety
    encircling you,
    caressing you, holding you?
What is this rich, resplendent protection
that embraces you,
    its heavy, gold-threaded majesty
    too dazzling for the human eye to bear?
Dear one,
    you are wrapped in the robes of God.

Psalm 9:10; 121

Your Wants

For to me, to live is Christ.

PHILIPPIANS 1:21 NIV

Yes, live in Me.
My Spirit is bigger
than the world around you.
I give you the full measure
of life's gifts. I give you
the full vocabulary
of heaven's poetry.
My gift is all music
of all eternity,
even the discordant phrases
and passages you find difficult.

Be strong and of good courage!
Trials are also gifts from Me,
changing you from one glory
to another. Never shrink back from your
high calling as an overcomer

in My kingdom.
    Live with Me above the void. Reach up beyond
    the stunted, measured human heights.
If you want to fly,
    come soar the heights with Me.
Your life is hid in the fortress
of My eye. You will not look to the world
    for what you want.
        Dear one!
I am what you want.

Hosea 14:4; Psalm 91:9–11; 1 John 4:4; James 1:2–3;
2 Samuel 22:2; Psalm 71:1; Deuteronomy 31:6

The Gift of the Second Mile

And whoever compels you to go one mile,
go with him two.

Matthew 5:41 NKJV

You are never so weary
that you cannot go the second mile,
never so humble
that you cannot bend a little lower;
you're never so bereft
that you have nothing else to give.

True, overcoming faith
does not scrape the edges of the bowl,
does not grapple, beg,
panhandle, or cajole for favor.
Faith does not scramble for bites of life,
nor hide from earthly blows.

Faith rises up in power and
supernatural mastery.
I give you *abundant life,*
and that includes heavenly
resources.
The child of God is empowered
for one more mile.
The first mile is for man,
the second one is for Me.

Hebrews 12:3, 13

Hidden Resentment

Let us go right in to God himself, with
true hearts fully trusting him to receive us
because we have been sprinkled with
Christ's blood to make us clean
and because our bodies have been
washed with pure water.

HEBREWS 10:22 TLB

You hide resentment in a forest of other
negative thoughts. You have been hurt, maligned.
You haven't been treated unfairly. You've been
stolen from, crushed, and cursed, but you shrug
a casual righteous shrug
and try not to think about it.
You are like one hopping barefoot on the frozen ice
while insisting your toes are warm.
The hurts rumble against you;
storms of anger assail your peace of mind,
and yet you seek to be a teacher of peace.
You zealously strive for a place in ministry.

Resentment, because it is hidden,
    is tangled in jealousy and a hunger
to control others.
    Talk to Me and release this resentment.
Trust Me with your secrets. I won't faint
at what you tell Me. *I am God. I know all.*
    Your fear of admitting
and confessing resentment
    keeps you sluggish, sick, and depressed.
You strive. You find fault with others.
You are difficult to get along with.
    Will you allow Me to calm your inner storm?
Allow Me to remove resentment and pour the balm
of My Spirit over the sores that have gathered
against you.
    Resentment is like a hangman's noose, choking
you with threats of death and loss.
    This is the hour. Take My hand and let Me
assure you
    that no matter what you've been through,
I turn all things to good.

Acts 17:30; Hebrews 12:14–15; Matthew 5:9; Romans 8:28

Come Back

Cease striving and know that I am God. . . .
"Repent therefore and return,
that your sins may be wiped away,
in order that times of refreshing
may come from the presence of the Lord."

Psalm 46:10; Acts 3:19 NASB

Why do you run from Me?
You flee into the dismal
night of fear,
you tremble at shadows,
you imagine enemies, and re-live
nightmares of the past.
I do not send you
fire-tongued horrors;
I do not prepare steamy, dark paths
on which you trip in murky potholes,
tormented by those around you,
by your work, your surroundings,
and others' problems. It is not I who
leads you along a road of worry

and emotional chaos. I have swallowed
the past in the sea of forgetfulness.
I am the champion of your future.

Love does not burn the soul
with unbearable trials.
Love liberates,
renews,
invigorates,
enlivens.
And I am your love.
Come back.

Psalm 46:1–2; 40:2; 17:7

When Patience Seems Impossible

Do not, therefore, fling away your fearless confidence, for it carries a great and glorious compensation of reward.

Hebrews 10:35 AMP

Steadfast patience and endurance may seem
impossible to attain in the flurry of life
and the pressures around you, but endurance
accomplishes the Father's will.
Patience is as possible as love.
My spirit imparts to you My very thoughts.
Know that everything concerning you
and your life is on schedule.
You're not too old.
You're not too young.
It's not too late.
You won't miss a thing.
I am always perfectly on time.
I am just and fair.

I return to you what the locusts
and cankerworms of the past
have devoured.
All that you've lost will be multiplied back
to you. You've just begun.
In My divine order of things,
right at this moment, you are in the best place
you could possibly be.

Hebrews 10:36; Psalm 27:8, 14; Joshua 13:1;
Psalm 31:15; Joel 2:25

Be Brave and Do Hard Things

And without faith it is impossible to please Him,
for he who comes to God must believe that He is,
and that He is a rewarder of those who seek Him.

HEBREWS 11:6 NASB

Stand up
 and take your place.
 Do the work I have called you to.
Pull down the strongholds—
 be brave, be strong!
Let Me teach you
 how to triumph in My will.
Let Me be the love
 and the joy
that empowers you to act.
  Beauty is yours,
  power is yours,

and peace that passes
all human cognizance
is yours!

Rise up. Seek Me and find Me.
The time is *now*.

Psalm 143:10; Philippians 4:7; Matthew 7:7–8

Omega Faith

He said to me:
"It is done.
I am the Alpha and the Omega,
the Beginning and the End.
To him who is thirsty
I will give to drink without cost
from the spring of the water of life."

Revelation 21:6 NIV

I am the Beginning.
I am the End.
You are very concerned with beginnings.
You hesitate to reach
the end.
I am the Alpha/beginning,
the Omega/end,
your all-in-all.
Do you want to stay
an Alpha person—
always at the starting line of faith?

Move, I say!
    Learn of Me. Absorb My Word.
I am your health, your energy: I bring you
    to a grand finish that is not the end,
not a place where you collapse,
    emptied out, done.
It is a place where you
    allow Me freely
    to live through you,
consummating My purposes
    and your destiny.

Feel the wind of trials
    and victories in Me.
I am the Finisher, the fulfilling Omega.
    Live in the Omega of your faith.
Discover joy in *all* things!
    Lift your eyes from the starting line
    and focus on all that lies before you—
new discoveries,
new victories,
new holy charges as

My intimate friend
who understands and moves
in great faith, accomplishing My will
on earth.

Hebrews 12:2; Ecclesiastes 7:8; Acts 20:24;
Isaiah 42:9; 41:22; Hebrews 13:21

Trust Is Wisdom, Wisdom Is Trust

Acquire wisdom;
And with all your acquiring,
get understanding.

Proverbs 4:7 NASB

Do not think of Me as a human being
with human failings.
I am neither vindictive, nor fickle.
Nor am I cruel, as is common with humans.
I am not limited by human actions,
ideas, or feelings. I am far greater
than human thoughts of Me.
People may lose, nations may lose,
even churches may lose, but I *never* lose.
I will not lose *you*. Ever.
Don't let outward appearances deceive you.
I always prevail, and so will you as you hold fast
and trust Me with each detail of your life.
Become established and unmovable in wisdom,

ever alert to the devices of the devil, who blinds
the children of the world with deception
designed to mutilate and destroy
all that is lovely and good.
I want you to prosper
and be in good health.
I want your soul strong.
I want you wise, filled
with understanding and the gifts of My Spirit.
My kingdom is filled with delights
for your soul. Be as a child and seek wisdom.
This gift is yours.

Isaiah 55:8–9; John 10:27–28; 2 Corinthians 2:11; 1 Peter 5:8;
3 John 3; 1 Corinthians 16:13

The Cheerful Heart

The cheerful heart has a continual feast.
Proverbs 15:15b NIV

When you groan in spiritual hunger,
you may try to feed yourself
with earthly foods,
bread, wine, meat, sweets—
but you will never be satisfied.
Recognize your desperate need for joy.

You cannot live fully without
My perfect joy,
and My Son died on the cross
to give you this gift
found in tender communion with Me.
Come feast with Me,
feast on our friendship—
experience the delight
of the refreshed heart;
enjoy the soul's peace,

laughter as pure as running waters,
    and know it is I who makes you happy
in spite of every sorrow and circumstance.
    My Spirit prepares
    a banquet of delights for you.
Your cheerful heart is your healing,
    your health,
and your calling.

Proverbs 15:13; 17:22; Philippians 4:11; Romans 8:18; John 15:11

The Secret Place of Strength

"I have loved you with
an everlasting love;
I have drawn you with loving-kindness."
JEREMIAH 31:3B NIV

My treasure, My beloved,
take My heart in yours!
How lovely is the dawn
of your tender love for Me.
I will be to you as the spring
with its fragrance and new blossoms,
I will cause your feet to dance
upon the eyelids of sorrow,
and you will sing new songs
upon a bed of spices in the aromatic Presence
of My Spirit.
I am in the rain,
and you are My forest of trees;
I am the sun,

and you are My garden of flowers.
I am eternal majesty,
and you are intimate with Me.
I kiss the top of your head.
I bless your face,
your body,
your soul.
I love you with a love
that shaped the universe.
Live in your spiritual intelligence.
Exercise your gift of creativity
to give your all to the life I've given you.
I am in you,
and you are in
My secret place of strength.

Song of Solomon 4:7; Psalm 16:11; 19:8; 31:23; 90:1; 90:17; Ephesians 3:17–19; 5:2; 1 Corinthians 15:54; Isaiah 28:5–6

Deliverance

Many are the afflictions of the righteous,
But the LORD delivers him out of them all.

PSALM 34:19 NKJV

I remove the evil thing
    from around your neck.
I utterly destroy the weapon
    formed against you.
I strengthen you on your bed
    of languishing.
I lift you out of danger
    and plant you in a place
of safety and contentment.
    Don't be so hungry for feral adventure,
for exploitable affection and bitter morsels
    of forbidden fruit
which rots in the morning sun.
    I want to give you a clear mind,
thoughts as clean and fresh as a summer rain.
    I want to remove the crooked dreams

and memories that tangle your mind.
I will fill you with higher vision
for I know your desires. You want relief
from the harshness of the world,
a place of safety
and someone to love you
unconditionally.
Oh, dear one, I give you these,
and more.
I will deliver you, for I work signs and wonders
in heaven and on earth.
I delivered Daniel from the power of the lions,
and I deliver you.
Be free NOW in My name
forever.

Isaiah 54:17; Romans 8:11; 2 Corinthians 5:17; Revelation 3:12; Psalm 3:3, 23:6; Matthew 10:8; Romans 8:28; Galatians 5:1; 2 Samuel 22:2; Jeremiah 1:8; Daniel 6:27

Stop Punishing Yourself

He rescues and he saves; he performs signs and wonders in the heavens and on the earth. He has rescued Daniel from the power of the lions.

DANIEL 6:27 NIV

Those self-hating words
you listen to
are like wild bears
ever growling and stalking you,
robbing your peace,
pulling you from your true place
in Me.
They jump out of the dark,
claw at your windows and doors,
roar until you wring your hands
and tear your hair,
and with their foul, hot breath

choking the air you breathe,
you become sick and feeble.
When will you chase these devils away?
When will you rise up and take your power?
You must no longer
punish yourself for the sins
of others
and for the shame of the past.

You must accept this Truth:
The past is gone,
finished.
I offer you a life
in a sweet and holy atmosphere
of continual blessing and mercy.
But you allow guilt and shame
to rule your thoughts
when you relish recounting
old losses and injustices,
and you invite the wild beasts
to torture their helpless prey.
BUT YOU ARE NOT HELPLESS.

You are full of promise
and crowned with might.
Conquer the bear within
and love yourself.

2 Peter 2:19; 1 Samuel 17:37; Proverbs 23:7; 16:3;
Song of Solomon 2:11; Psalm 34:17–18; Romans 12:21;
2 Corinthians 10:5

You Are My Heart's Delight

As the bridegroom rejoices over the bride,
So your God will rejoice over you.

Isaiah 62:5b NASB

The bridegroom rejoices over the bride because he is in love. I am the Bridegroom and I love you, My bride.

Together you and I are one. We are stars and sun at the wedding feast,

our light so dazzling it blinds all else. I delight in your love.

Never feel forsaken, for I will not let you fall; I will never leave you alone.

If your courage in life wanes, I empower you, I lift you up

new,

tough,

beautiful,

and pure

before all heaven and earth,
because you are Mine and you love Me—
And because you love Me, I encircle you in the light of My love, O bride, O beloved.
Weep no more, for you are blessed of Me and My heart's delight.

Joshua 1:5; Jeremiah 30:17; 1 John 1:5–7; Psalm 91:14; Isaiah 65:19; Proverbs 12:22b; Isaiah 62:4

Find Yourself

For whoever finds me finds life.
Proverbs 8:35a NIV

You are accustomed to seeking yourself
in others,
    in achievements and labors
and in diversions
    unsuitable for you.
If you do not see My goodness in you,
    you will be unsatisfied with your life
and always be searching for the unattainable.
    You are who you are
as I have made you,
    and in Me you will not want
for any good thing.
    I feed the spider, I feed the porpoise,
I protect the hawk and the sparrow,
    and I watch over you.
I give you *good.*

I create goodness
in you.
Find Me
and you will find
yourself.

2 Chronicles 6:41; 2 Thessalonians 1:11

LORD, I'M AFRAID

You have considered my trouble;
You have known my soul
in adversities.

PSALM 31:7 NKJV

Lord, sometimes I'm so afraid
my skin grows cold
and I can hardly breathe.
I feel so helpless.
I'm afraid of so many things—
of certain people, of being alone,
of death, pain,
not having enough money. . . .
Lord, the list never ends.
I just can't help myself.

I am your refuge and your fortress,
your God on whom you can rely.
Do you not know that
in Me you are
safe?
When you live in My shelter,
you are in a stable place;
you are in the shadow of the Almighty,
whose power no enemy can withstand.
Be filled with My Spirit
so you can rise above your human
strength and live in My
supernatural strength.
I will deliver you
from all traps and snares.
I will cover you with the holy feathers
of My protecting wings.
My Holy Spirit within you will
convince you of your place
of safety.
In the place of safety
you will not be afraid
of destruction,
real or imagined.

Though you may observe the world
stumbling and falling around you,
you will walk in your integrity,
empowered by My Spirit,
and you will be unscathed.
Make a home for your heart
in the secret place of the Most High,
the place where you were born
to live.

Psalm 91:1–7

Prayer for Greatness

He has shown you, O man,
what is good;
And what does the LORD
require of you
But to do justly,
To love mercy,
And to walk humbly
with your God?

MICAH 6:8 NKJV

Lord, help me
to come forth like Lazarus,
sing in prison like Paul,
pray with wisdom like Solomon,
dance like David,
love like Ruth,
be faithful like Daniel,
courageous like David ,
valiant like Deborah,
have the patience of Job;

worthy of praise like
the Proverbs 31 woman—
I want to be great
in Your eyes.

If you would have the greatness
of a hero—
would you also bear the suffering?
The greatest is the least
in My kingdom,
and true greatness becomes
the lowly servant.
As for you,
you will walk
in your integrity,
and in you
I will be well pleased.
You will bless
the name of the Lord and
bring Me much honor and glory.
We will go forth as One.
That is greatness.

Matthew 18:1–4; 23:11; Psalm 103:1; Matthew 5:16;
2 Corinthians 3:18

Good Morning, Beloved

"As the Father loved me, I also have loved you; abide in My love."

John 15:9

He brought me to the
banqueting house,
And His banner over me was love.

Song of Solomon 2:4 NKJV

Every morning
　　My compassion greets you
with a song of love.
　　The morning ensemble of stars
sing together, exulting in the new day;
　　the angels rejoice in their choir of perfect
harmony. I am THE Morning Star. I shine
　　on you with life, newness, beauty, and
holy strength moment by moment.
　　Lift up your eyes and see

the new mercies awaiting you right now.
Embrace what is yours.
I give you all you require
to feed the needs of your every hour;
I invigorate every muscle and fiber
of your being, I fill your eyes, ears
and every nerve with acute awareness—
Light and Life are Mine and you are Mine.
This day, which I have made, is My gift to you.
The work I have called you
to accomplish today is My work given to you.
Arise!
The Morning Star has risen in your heart,
and there are immense worlds
ready for you to discover.
Accept and seize
the multitudinous spectrum of My promises
heaped before you this day.
Your light rushes to you on angel wings,
embracing and illuminating all that is yours.

Revelation 22:16; John 12:46; Lamentations 3:23–24;
Psalm 74:16; Ephesians 6:10; John 14:12;
1 Corinthians 15:58; 2 Peter 1:4, 19

The Gift of the Yoke

Take My yoke upon you, and learn from Me,
for I am gentle and humble in heart, and
you shall find rest for your souls.

MATTHEW 11:29 NASB

I will never hurt you
nor afflict you, My beloved child.
I remove the mental labor
and the agony you suffer,
and I give you rest.
When the turmoil of your mind
feels like a hundred hurricanes,
and your soul feels crumpled
like old papers to throw out,
come. Let Me hold you.
Let Me kiss your nose,
you are safe with Me.
You are yoked to Me.

I do not leave you helpless
to battle the hounds of hell alone,

nor have I left you
to battle your *self* alone.
    Hush now,
    My yoke holds you tight to Me.

O learn of Me and listen.
    You can't hear Me when you yank
at the yoke.
    My holy outstretched hand
    is mightier than the wrinkled fist
of the world. Know that the impact of righteousness,
    which you inherited in Me,
is peace within and without,
    confident trust forever.
If you could see the jeweled yoke
    you wear on your neck, perhaps
your crown would not seem so heavy.
    We are yoked together,
you and I—yoked
    like two oxen pulling a cart.
        But dear one, you seem to forget
        it's I who do the pulling,
        not you.

Matthew 11:28–30; Psalm 38:4; Isaiah 32:17; 30:15; Psalm 56:3

THE GIFT OF HOPE

For we were saved in this hope,
but hope that is seen is not hope;
for why does one still hope for what he sees?
But if we hope for what we do not see,
we eagerly wait for it with perseverance.

ROMANS 8:24–25 NKJV

I am Hope.
I give you more than future glory,
I am your *present* glory.
I understand when you are uncertain
about My will,
when you cry out in despair
for the life of a loved one,
the mending of a relationship
that has gone awry like a sprung coil,
or for physical healing.
Do not lose heart,
do not lose hope,
because I hear
and I answer.

My ears are not closed to your voice;
I know your heart, I hear you,
but My perfect will does not flop like fish
on the sand. I cannot change
because you insist
you know better than I.

Allow My written Word,
which throbs
with the power of hope,
to enter your mind and body
like fresh blood in your veins,
new life in your thoughts.
Your faith is the very substance,
that is, the express image,
of what you hope for.
The unseen answer is
your present assurance
and evidence of the fulfillment
of My loving promises to you.
You *have* what you have asked for.
Take My mind, My wisdom,
My knowledge, My understanding,
these My gifts to you,
to give you hope,

for your hope is My Son,
the One who builds your mansion even now.
Tell Me, how will you recognize the sound
of His holy hammer and chisel
without hope?
Caress the sister of love,
which is My gift of hope,
for you have not been guided
by human wisdom, no.
I have taught you by My Holy Spirit,
so now! Bulldoze the mountains,
sound the battle cry,
prepare to win!
Your hope of glory
is Christ *in* you.

1 Peter 1:16; Psalm 99:3; Hebrews 7:26; Luke 11:13;
Hebrews 11:1; Matthew 5:8; Colossians 1:27

The Gift of Godliness

Discipline yourself for the purpose of godliness.

1 Timothy 4:7b NASB

Consider yourself in training.
Every day you must exercise
for spiritual fitness.
As the love of Christ controls,
urges, and impels you,
you will take one step at a time
and learn to walk by faith
and not by sight.
Then, swift and smooth,
you will be running not on blistered hopes
and aching schemes for a better life,
but you will aim yourself sure and steady
on a straight course,
preparing for the race
that has already been won for you.

The tutoring of My Spirit
is not simply to prepare you for
the rigors and contests of the human will,
nor for the tenuous rewards of your labor, no.
The extra mile I assign you
can only be tackled in the power of My Spirit.
Your human strength is not sufficient.
Your courage dwells in the integrity of your faith,
for I vindicate and strengthen the righteous.
I am your power. I am your courage.

Psalm 31:24; Matthew 5:41–42; 2 Corinthians 5:7;
Matthew 28:18; Ezekiel 36:27; Zechariah 4:6

Your Finest Hour

"Be strong and courageous; do not be afraid nor dismayed before the king of Assyria, nor before all the multitude that is with him; for there are more with us than with him. With him is an arm of flesh, but with us is the LORD our God, to help us and to fight our battles."

2 CHRONICLES 32:7–8 NKJV

This is your finest hour.
I have prepared you for this battle.
Put on your courage. Enter into the inner court
of My Spirit where My Son strengthens
you. I have prepared a place for you—
enter into and share the joyous power
that surpasses human ability
because you live in Me
and I live in you.
Be about your Father's business!

Be steadfast, unmovable, abounding in
the work I've called you to.
My Presence goes before you,

and no interior battle is too fierce
to confront head-on, full-faced
and victorious.
Take your armor and the oil of gladness
and follow Me in confidence,
for I cause you to triumph
in My kingdom and My work.
Asking without confidence
is like a gift without a giver.
I am Ruler of all heaven and earth,
your Creator,
your strength,
your only path to greatness.
Remember, the one greatest in My kingdom
is the least.
Press on!

Matthew 25:23; Deuteronomy 31:6; 1 Corinthians 15:58;
Hebrews 4:16; John 15:4, 11, 15–16; Exodus 34:14;
Matthew 11:11

ALLOWING YOURSELF TO CHANGE

You have begun to live the new life,
in which you are being made new and are becoming
like the One who made you.
This new life brings you the true knowledge of God.

COLOSSIANS 3:10 NCV

Steady yourself.
Give your impatient struggles to Me!
Give Me the right to be in control of all things.
I shall change you and renew your strength.
You shall be lifted up on giant wings
and mounted close to God,
as eagles mount up to the sun.
You shall run and not become fatigued;
you shall walk and not collapse.
Your soul is possessed in your patience.
When you hope in Me, utterly rely on Me,
when you foresee in the Spirit your answers
from Me,

and unconditionally trust My decisions,
you will experience an amazing transformation:
You *change.*
Where you were once impatient, short-tempered,
riddled with frustration and nervous anxiety,
you find yourself at peace!
Yes, at peace! You are no longer alarmed or depressed
because of evildoers who prosper. You no longer
gnash your teeth at the wickedness
of the world—
your prayers are confident! You take your honored
position as My child who has My ear,
and you pray
with assurance in the power of My Spirit—
knowing,
trusting,
believing,
resting
in My divine promise of imminent answers.

Isaiah 40:31; Psalm 37:9; Philippians 1:6; 1 Thessalonians 5:24; Luke 21:19; 2 Corinthians 3:18; 5:17

When You Need Strength

Hear my cry, O God;
Attend to my prayer.
From the end of the earth
I will cry to You,
When my heart is overwhelmed;
Lead me to the rock that
is higher than I.

PSALM 61:1–2 NKJV

Beloved one, I furnish you
with the grit and authority by My Spirit
in the inner chambers of your being
for you to go forth fearlessly in command
of all I've given you to do and be.
Discontent will bite like fleas,
but the confidence I give you
is a heavenly kiss of My love
and assurance.
I make you strong because I am strong.

Working out the snares and sorrows of life
in your natural strength
will erode your energy, rob your vitality.
You need spiritual vigor, and I am here to fulfill
your every need.
I have opened many doors for you to enter.
Walk through them one by one.
Do not be deterred
when the blessings you receive from Me
are accompanied by jealous demons
with mouths of thorns and eyes like spikes.
Do not bargain with these devils,
or clasp their hands
in a naïve effort to avoid conflict and make
friends
of the enemy.
Concentrate on the task I give you and your
abiding friendship
with Me. Rule your heart.
Remind yourself, beloved child of Mine,
I am the light of your life.
I save you from yourself.

Daniel 10:19; Ephesians 3:16; Psalm 18:2; Ephesians 6:19;
Revelation 3:8; John 10:7; Ephesians 5:8

Waiting for a Mate

And the LORD God said, "It is not good that a man should be alone; I will make him a helper comparable to him."

Genesis 2:18 NKJV

Lord, it's not easy!
I try, I brave it out, I pray.
I have not fallen
yet,
but it's depressing
not to be cherished except
by You.
People rush through my world
like shadows.
The dogs of past hurts
growl from behind my bed
at night. Where is the beautiful
mate You've chosen for me?
The clock is ticking, Lord.
How much longer must I
be alone?

Beloved,
I hold your life in My hand.
I want to lift you to greater heights
in Me, beyond the hallways of waiting
for your mate. I want to show you
great and wondrous things in My kingdom.
I want to build in you a strength
that cannot fail.
I am your lover and friend.
I cure your pains and sorrows.
I open My hand to satisfy you
with favor. Loneliness shall not overwhelm you,
for I rescue you
from behind the high walls you build
to protect an anxious soul.
I tell you this so that you will reach out
beyond yourself for more of Me.
Let Me give you the fountain of revelation and joy.
Let me open the heavens
before you.
I have answered your prayers.

Isaiah 41:13; Psalm 146:8–9; 149:4; 147:3; 149:5; John 15:11;
Matthew 3:16; Revelation 19:11; Deuteronomy 29:29

The Beauty of Praise

O Lord, open my lips, and my mouth
will declare your praise.

PSALM 51:15 NIV

When you accept
the grace I give to you
and can at last
give Me praise in every circumstance,
come. My court waits
for you.
Praise Me in all things.
Praise Me in the silence of your night,
praise Me in the crashing noon,
praise Me in silence
and in awe.
Praise Me in thankful sobs,
praise Me in noise and laughter.
Praise Me with harp, lyre, guitar,
keyboard, dance, and drum.
Praise the Lord, O My own!

Praise Me with your boundless
creative gifts. Praise Me in your emptiness.
I have opened the gates.
Enter as leading a measureless
procession of jeweled and robed saints.
Pass the tall carved pillars
along the golden promenade
to My sacred courts
with your songs of thanksgiving
and praise.
Dance and song and gladness
fill My house,
and your praise fills My heart.

Deuteronomy 8:10; Psalm 33:2; 100:4

Remove Your Limitations

"For the mountains may be removed
and the hills may shake,
but My lovingkindness will not be removed from you,
and My covenant of peace will not be shaken,"
says the LORD *who has compassion on you.*

ISAIAH 54:10 NASB

Do not impose limitations on Me.
Do not lock Me away
inside the gates
of your fears and habits.
Secretly, you believe
that you will always
live a life of lack, and this is like
binding yourself to a burning post
and asking why it's so hot.
You are called to live a life of goodness
and abundance. I am able
to meet all your requirements.

You can do all things through Me.
I say, multiply your talents,
embrace the knowledge I've given you,
grow in the Spirit!
It's time to discard your old ways of thinking.
I, your Father in heaven,
know your needs before you know them.
Today be lifted up
above the deceptions of yesterday.
Receive new vision,
new understanding,
new power through My Word.
Never put a limit on the blessings
I have for you.
It takes courage
and it takes time
to take more of Me.

Romans 5:10; Matthew 6:8, 32; Isaiah 54:17

Lord, How Do I Resist Sin?

Blessed is the man who endures
temptation; for when he has been approved,
he will receive the crown of life which
the LORD has promised to those who love Him.

JAMES 1:12 NKJV

Lord, give me the power
to turn away from temptation
and to stand for what I know
is right. I want to be strong
and not sin, but it's such
a battle. Please help me.

Take heart, dear one.
Urges of the soul
scream for attention,
but you will never
be satisfied with sin.

You will not be at peace
with worldly substitutes
for sublime joy in Me.
I am woven into the texture
of your being,
and you are woven into Me.
Sin is at war with your true nature,
the nature of God in you.
Sin is unnatural,
out of harmony with yourself
and with Me.
I give you power
to overcome.
For greater is the pulse
of My presence
within you than
the enemy's temptations.
Lock My words in your heart
where they will protect you
and sear deep into your mind.
You are an overcomer.

You can accomplish all things
through Me for I am
your life.

Luke 17:21; Romans 8:9–11; 1 John 4:4; Romans 6:2;
Psalm 119:11; Revelation 2:17; Galatians 2:20; Luke 10:19

Lord, How Do I Get Your Favor?

When a man's ways
please the Lord,
He makes even his enemies to be
at peace with him.

Proverbs 16:7 NKJV

I'm always trying to please
someone. In fact, Lord,
I've spent most of my life
trying to please others.
I crave approval and gratification,
but it's not always there.
Show me how I can win
Your stamp of approval.
How can I know I have
found favor with You?

Look at My Son Jesus.
He pleased very few people,
yet He was perfect love made human.
He was sinless, loving, and good.
He pleased Me in every way
and was obedient to the point
of a grisly death by crucifixion.
He is your example, your High Priest,
your Teacher, and your Savior.
Favor through Him is My free gift
to you. It's called grace.
If you have My favor,
there is no need to strive
for fickle human approval.
Am I not able to give you favor among
others as I purpose?
Be at peace. You work at earning
love and favor like a bird trying to flutter
its wings in a violent storm.
You only exhaust yourself.
I show you what is good
and what is required of you:
justice, love of mercy, and walking
humbly with Me. You are not

of this world. You are Mine and you belong
to Me. Those who are of this world
hunger and crave and are never satisfied.
Love Me with your entire being.
Make My heart glad and you will know gladness
beyond compare.
You'll know you have My favor.

Matthew 3:17; John 8:29; 12:45; 1 John 2:15–17; Micah 6:8; Matthew 5:3; Deuteronomy 10:12–13

Lord, Why Do Some People Seem More Blessed Than Others?

My heart is stricken and
withered like grass . . .

Psalm 102:4 NKJV

I can't seem to overcome
the trials of my life, and yet
I look around me and see
other people who don't suffer
as I do. They seem to lead happy,
prosperous lives. I can't understand
why everything I do
seems to wind up in failure,
when other people seem
to succeed. I wonder why
I'm not blessed like everybody
else. After all, I'm a Christian.

Your troubles need not possess you,
and your heart need not
bask in such desolate darkness.
Let My Spirit teach you
to triumph in your troubles
so you can enjoy your life in Me.
You must learn to take
your authority in My name. You must learn
to stand tall and wage war against
self-pity and envy. You must take hold
of the blessings and the power
My Son gave to you by His death on the cross.
The Holy Spirit raised My Son Jesus,
from the dead, and this same Spirit dwells in you,
restoring and empowering your mortal,
short-lived, perishable self in Me.
"Abba," you cry out, and I answer,
"Yes, child, I am here for you." I am here
to strengthen you and lift you
out of the claws of self-defeat.
Quiet your anxious soul until you feel
the gentle breath of God strengthening you
to take a stand for the success that is
ordained for you. Hardship is not a curse,
but a tool to reach endurance, faith, integrity,

and maturity of character (do you want to remain a baby?).

Be strong, be strong, I say, and take your favor.

John 14:1, 27; Romans 5:3–4; 8:5, 9; 8:14–17; 8:11; Hebrews 12:1–3

THE GIFT OF THE NARROW GATE

"Enter by the narrow gate; for wide is the gate
and broad is the way that leads to destruction,
and there are many who go in by it. Because narrow
is the gate and difficult is the way which leads to life,
and there are few who find it."

MATTHEW 7:13-14 NKJV

Don't consider your own pain as trivial.
I hold your hand
and guide you with My gentleness.
Your emotions will not defeat you,
and you shall not be swallowed by your failures,
nor the failures of those around you
as you allow My gentleness to minister to you
and learn to extract the precious
from the powerless.
There is no power in fear,
so choose the narrow gate,
the one you must shrink yourself

to the size of a child to get through,
like threading yourself through
the tiny eye of a needle.
I promise you, when you have come through,
when you have fought the good fight,
won the war with your emotions,
and broken through from without
and from within,
you will come upon a heavenly throng
with their voices resounding in cheers.
My Son stands in the midst of them,
His arms outstretched to you,
welcoming you to victory.
Oh, beloved, I live behind the narrow gate,
for the cross of Calvary is the narrow road.
The way may be filled with hardship,
but at its end
you walk in My soul.

Psalm 18:35; Romans 8:1; 1 Thessalonians 2:7; Luke 13:24; Matthew 16:24–25; John 12:26; Psalm 73:24

The Life of the Disciple

Choose you this day whom ye will serve.

JOSHUA 24:15 KJV

I have made it easy for you to *receive* My love,
but the *walk* of love is not easy. It means denying
yourself, turning the other cheek, putting others'
needs before your own, harnessing your
selfish desires,
dying to your natural self.

The life of the disciple is a separated, holy one,
given entirely to Me. Tightly united with Me,
in complete surrender to Me and My will,
wisdom, joy, and supernatural peace
cascade out of your innermost being
like rivers of rushing waters.
You must understand that the godly person
is consumed by My love
and presence. You do nothing selfishly.
You don't strive for even the tiniest shred

of personal gain. *For you to live is Christ.*
To be My disciple is to know and choose
to walk in My love.
Everything I am and all I do is in love.
Choose love today.
Choose to come to Me for more than
your private wants and needs.
Choose to leave your personal baggage
at the eye of the needle.
Pass through and fall before My throne
and worship.

Romans 12:1; 6:17–19

God's Thoughts Toward You

For I know the thoughts that I think toward you, says the LORD, thoughts of peace and not of evil, to give you a future and a hope.

JEREMIAH 29:11 NKJV

I want you to hear My thoughts toward you
so the gates of your ears are unlocked
and your mind is illuminated
to know and understand
the riches of your inheritance in Me.
I want you to realize the incomparably great power
that is in you because you are Mine.
My thoughts of you hold you snug and safe
in My eternal plan.

Release yourself from the prison of human reasoning. Do not think you were called to live a life of heartache and endless troubles. I heal your wounds and release you from

the shackles of a troubled life. Choose My arms
of love from this day on. No longer accept
a life under the oppressor's yoke.
You will no more be a slave to ungodly lusts
and lack of self-respect. Your shame is gone.
My loving thoughts toward you
break off the handcuffs of pride that bruise
your wrists and waste your days.
Don't be like a frantic cat clawing in water
with self-defense and excuses.
I am the One who defends you.
I rescue you. I hold you tight in My arms
and keep you safe.
I want you to open the eyes of your heart
and see My thoughts toward you.
You cannot separate
My loving thoughts from your daily life.
When I think of you
I see you crowned in mercy
and wearing your crown with dignity.
When I think of you
I see you surrendered to Me, taking Me at My
word.

I see you loving My Word.
I see you taking up your cross and following Me,
loving My thoughts.
I see you loving My love
and loving Me.

John 15:9; Romans 8:35; Isaiah 26:3; Jeremiah 30:17;
Ephesians 1:18–20; 3:17–19; 1 John 3:1; Romans 5:8

THE GIFT OF STRENGTH

O my Strength, I sing praise to you;
you, O God, are my
fortress, my loving God.

PSALM 59:17 NIV

When you ask for help
I am there.
When you need strength
I am there.
I want to see you live in strength,
and less in ravenously seeking signs
outside yourself.
There is one miracle you need now:
the miracle of inner strength.
When you are strong
you possess all things—
dignity, solid footing, worth, vision.
Be strong, dear one!
Be strong in My strength.

New health, new wisdom,
new understanding,
new success are
ahead for you.
With My strength you cannot fail.

Psalm 91:14–16; Ephesians 3:16; 2 Corinthians 12:9–10

Lord, How Am I Supposed to Forgive?

O my God, I trust in You;
Let me not be ashamed;
Let not my enemies triumph over me.

PSALM 25:2 NKJV

Lord, I want to be forgiving—
but it's hard.
I feel hurt and angry,
and it seems hypocritical
to simply mouth the words
I'm *supposed* to feel.
In my heart there is not
one drop of forgiveness.
I want to fight
and get back what I've lost.
How can I forgive
and ask your blessing
on those who have hurt me?

Dear one, I am not heartless and
demanding,
and I do not ask you
to deny your emotions,
nor do I ask you to mask
your hurts from Me.
Your Lord and Savior
hears and sees
and understands.
I have compassion.
Come bathe in the healing,
refreshing balm of My love.
Let Me caress
your hurts.
Let Me take the wrongs done you
on My own body,
which I gave for you
at the cross.
I, too, was treated badly.
I was beaten, whipped, spit upon.
Nails were struck through my flesh;
I was left hanging—
innocent of every sin.

Give Me the pain you feel,
and I will save you
from its lasting sting.
I forgive you of every wrong,
and you have the power
to forgive, also.
Release yourself
into My rest
and pray that
the wicked will forsake their way
and unrighteous persons their plans.
I know your adversities,
and My Spirit, who is in you, will guide you
and ease the struggle
until you are completely free.

Colossians 3:13; Mark 11:25; Hebrews 9:14; John 16:15; Hebrews 2:17; 1 Peter 2:21–22; Isaiah 55:7; Psalm 31:7

My Counsel—Your Crown

I will instruct you and teach you
in the way you should go;
I will counsel you and watch over you.

Psalm 32:8 NIV

Today
you have much to learn.
See the joy
set before you.
Take the crown
I give you
and wear it with the confidence
only My chosen understand.
Do not be held back
by hesitation and
those fright-filled pauses
you call concern.
I give you confidence,
surety,

a new personal bearing
    that raises your shoulders
and lifts your chin.
    I give vitality to your step.
Wisdom will stream from the words
    of your mouth.
You are wearing My purposes,
My plans.

Do not trouble yourself
    with temporary losses.
I am forever a giving God.
    See the permanent.
    Love the permanent.
    Live in the permanent.

Psalm 23:6; 103:4; Proverbs 14:18; 1 Kings 18:21; Romans 8:28

The Gift of Energy

Do you not know? Have you not heard?
The Everlasting God, the LORD, the Creator
of the ends of the earth
Does not become weary or tired.

ISAIAH 40:28 NASB

Because My understanding is infinite,
unsearchable,
inscrutable,
because My love is life
and holy energy
forever,
I heal your broken heart
and bind up your wounds
when you cry out to Me.

There are no outcasts in My kingdom,
no weary, beleaguered, undone,
pathetic pariahs
for whom the angels jeer or sob.
I count the stars and give names to each of them;

I count the tears
on your chin, My beloved one.
My eye is on you when your foot is slow.
Love is strength,
and I am able to support you;
I open the palms of My hands
to make a path
for your slow foot to run upon with ease.

I bring the wicked to their knees
in the garbage heaps of their pursuits.
I am He who does not restrain lightning
from striking My adversaries;
I breathe into the sky
so that clouds and rain are formed;
I create snow like wool
and command it to shroud the land;
I scatter frost like ashes
and call to the tumultuous storm,
Be still.
How can the natural abilities of the thing created
stand in defiance
before their everlasting Creator?

When My children quake and grow weak
in the knees,
    they cry out to Me and I answer.
    I increase their strength.
I empower My weary ones with courage.
    I energize and increase wisdom.
When you trust in My strength
    to accomplish your many works
and to overcome your many trials,
    you will mount up with wings like eagles.
My strength empowers
    the legs of My chosen ones
to run and not exhaust themselves,
    to tread steadily and not become weary.

Young lions,
    though they are strong in the forest,
become hungry and weak and have no voice
    to cry out in prayer. It is not to these
I give My power and renewed energy,
    but to *you,* My own,
to *you.*

Psalm 147:3–5; Romans 11:33; Job 37:2–7; Isaiah 40:28–31;
Psalm 34:10

The Hiding Place

"Behold, I have inscribed you on the palms of My hands;
Your walls are continually before Me."

Isaiah 49:16 NASB

I hold you in the hollow of My hand.
You can make this secret, holy place
your home,
if you choose.
Day and night you may rest
in the hollow of My hand,
where no storm or quake can disturb.

To rest in My hand!
This is the dream of all humankind,
though many do not know
their quest for protection
is a hunger for Me.
My hand is always open to you.

Your place with Me is safe—
your hiding place
in My hand,
where I want to hold you
for always.
There is no better place
than here.

John 10:28; Psalm 18:3; 75:8–10; 91:9–12; Revelation 3:8;
Isaiah 25:4

THE QUIET HEART

"In quietness and trust is your strength."

ISAIAH 30:15 NASB

Quiet your mind.
Listen for the small desires
of your heart and Mine.
Listen for our thoughts
to meld together,
forming a perfect union.
With Me, you will discover
invisible strains of heavenly glory
in the smallest breath of life.
Nothing is insignificant to Me,
and I open the eyes of your spirit
to see into the realm of My will,
where you will worship with
the angels and the heavenly host.
Listen to the sweet urgings
of My Spirit for this new day.
It is the restless, equipped heart

that demands the spectacular,
the sensational, the loud and showy.
Listen for the silence
of My voice.
Cherish the simple.
I work slowly and do a perfect work
in you. If you do not love the rudimentary
and the plain, how will you be prepared
for the majestic and sublime?
Do not ferment in the bustle of the world
around you. Love is simple, not complex;
let your passion for Me
soften the harried edges of your soul,
and be quiet.

Psalm 4:4; John 15:11; Philippians 1:6; Numbers 9:8;
Romans 2:7

Your New Day

"Arise, shine; for your light has come,
And the glory of the LORD has risen upon you."

ISAIAH 60:1 NASB

Awake, dear one.
    Clothe yourself with strength.
Awake, and take the robes I give you.
Awake, and live this day in power
    and integrity.
Don't hide the loveliness of My truth
    in your shoe or your back pocket,
but wear it openly like an expensive coat.
    My Spirit of truth
    makes you to shine
with My Presence.
    I will give and give
and give and give
    to you today.
Your eyes will be opened,
your body strengthened,

your mind refreshed,
and your heart cleansed.
    Walk in My light.
    I am your Light.
        Arise!

---

1 Thessalonians 5:8; Matthew 13:43; 1 John 1:7

Led by My Spirit

"But you shall receive power when the Holy Spirit has come upon you; and you shall be My witnesses both in Jerusalem, and in all Judea and Samaria, and even to the remotest part of the earth."

Acts 1:8 NASB

I am He who fashioned the heavens
    and stretched the waters into seas;
I speak to you day and night
    if you have ears to hear.
I will show you great and wonderful things,
    for I have created you for such a time
as this, and My purposes.
    Do not lose your way trying to
make happen
    that which you are not called to do.
To labor at even the tiniest detail
    without Me
is unnatural and unbearably futile.
    Listen for My Spirit's leading, for
He is your Helper.

I have many skies for you to fly,
many valleys for you to cross,
many mountains to remove.
You will reap much
if you faint not.
Be bold, for My Spirit releases His gifts
into your life. You will love this calling.
You will see My hand move, and
you will not cease to be surprised
by joy.
Come boldly before My throne of grace,
bring to Me your gifts, your prayers;
bring My joy with you
and change your world.

Ezekiel 36:27; Joel 2:28; Matthew 3:11; John 14:17;
2 Corinthians 3:6; Luke 18:1; Romans 12:12; Galatians 6:9;
Matthew 28:19–20

The Disturbed Heart

The LORD is in His holy temple;
the LORD's throne is in heaven;
His eyes behold, His eyelids test the sons of men.

PSALM 11:4 NASB

I rule the surging sea;
I still the turmoil of nations,
and I make the massive voice of the strong
a mere whimper.
I rebuke the wind and the lightning,
the hail, snow, and rain
do My bidding.
Who has gathered up the wind
in the hollow of his hands?
Who has wrapped up the waters
in his cloak?
Who has established
all the ends of the earth?
What is his name?
Tell me if you know.
I, the Lord of all,

gave the sea its boundary,
I marked the foundations
of the earth—
and I can quiet your disturbed heart.

Allow Me.

Psalm 65:5–7; 107:29; Job 38; Matthew 8:26; Proverbs 30:4; Philippians 2:5; 1 Corinthians 2:16

Hang On!

The Lord is not slow about His promise,
as some count slowness,
but is patient toward you,
not wishing for any to perish
but for all to come to repentance.

2 PETER 3:9 NASB

How deep is your wound, dear one?
Anchor your spirit in Mine:
  I will rejuvenate you,
I will pour warm oil of inner strength
  upon you.
Your concern for the future
  beats at you like driving rain
  on a blossoming flower.
Soon the torrents will bow your head,
  you'll lose your fragrance
  and you will become
    wilted,
    soggy,
    frayed.

Your storm of worry is not ordained by Me.
 Won't you end this tempest and
 live the winged life above the cares
that rob your soul of joyous flight?
 You struggle to manipulate life's
 eventualities and your efforts frustrate you
 because you cannot control God
or the world.
  You can *know* the mind of Christ,
 but you cannot *control* the mind of Christ.
No longer count the scars, but count
 My promises to you and your
 answered prayers. You are stronger
than you realize.

Matthew 6:27; James 4:3; 1 Corinthians 2:16; Isaiah 41:10;
Psalm 36:7; Malachi 4:2; 2 Corinthians 6:2; Psalm 3:3

MORE THAN PATIENCE

"Then you will call, and the LORD will answer;
You will cry, and He will say, 'Here I am.'"

ISAIAH 58:9A NASB

Yes, it may seem that I am not answering
soon enough.
You find yourself in the valley
of waiting and
you feel as though you're trapped,
with no way out of your anxiety.
Do you think you can sit on the hot coals
of anxiety and not be blistered?
Learn to laugh.
Learn to hear the Lord's laughter. I do not
wince with worry, nor grind My teeth
in impatience.

I have promised to answer you,
and I never go back on a promise.

I will surely answer you;
but dear one,
I answer in My time,
not yours.

Isaiah 25:9; Psalm 91:15; 126:2–3; 33:21; Proverbs 7:1–2; Isaiah 65:24

Love Them, Help Them, Bring Them Home

"Is this not the fast which I choose,
To loosen the bonds of wickedness,
To undo the bands of the yoke,
And to let the oppressed go free,
And break every yoke?"

ISAIAH 58:6 NASB

Beloved,
touch and bless the world with hands
that have been kissed
by My love.
Embrace the ugly and the beautiful,
submitting all to Me
as a timeless bouquet.
Lift up the heads which hang
in despair;
open the woeful gates,
that the King of Glory

may come into the dark places
where pessimism has governed
and affliction ruled. Present Me.
Sound the call.
Caress the downtrodden,
the vexed, the homeless,
the proud, and the terrible.
Call forth your great minds of the day,
the ones who unfurl their inflated words
like playthings valued by fools and mutts.
I tell you, they cry out for Me and know
it not.
Blow the horn, I say.
Be loving to the unloving.
Be strong for the weak.
Let your arms extend beyond your borders.
Kiss this hour of My anointing
and bring My children home.
Bring them home.

---

1 Thessalonians 3:12; Galatians 5:13; Matthew 5:43–46;
Isaiah 12:4; Romans 15:1; Isaiah 58:6–8, 10; Joel 2:1;
Proverbs 9:5

The Mighty Overcomer

For whatever is born of God overcomes the world.

1 JOHN 5:4A NASB

Is there a prison strong enough
to chain your boundless spirit?
Is there a lie cunning enough
to vanquish your great heart?
Where the Spirit of the Lord is,
there is liberty,
exultation,
creative power,
and you can do all things
through Christ
who strengthens you.
There are no barbs
deadly enough to thwart your faith,
no raging wolves vigorous enough
to tear apart your joy,

no thieves shrewd enough
    to purloin My gifts to you.

Greater is the Spirit of God within you
    than any sinister plot in the world.
You have the authority
    to continually
live in sovereign liberty and glory
    as I infuse you with My strength,
because you were born
    to be victorious.

2 Corinthians 3:17; Philippians 4:13; 2 Timothy 1:7;
1 John 5:4–5

YOUR RICHES IN ME

If . . . God clothes the grass
of the field, which is here today,
and tomorrow is thrown into the fire,
how much more will he clothe you,
O you of little faith!
Life is more than food, and the body
more than clothes.

LUKE 12:28, 23

Be rich in Me.
    Be treasure-laden,
wear spiritual finery:
    take wisdom, humility, gentleness . . .
Possess the gem of wisdom,
polished and lacquered.
    Be garbed in the opulent clothing
of intelligence and wise choices
    embroidered with the golden strands
    of patience and suffering.
Wear on your hands

the precious stones
of humility and trials overcome.
Reach to the splendor of God
and let your hands, which are now sparkling
clean and powerful,
hold and help those
in unlit holes of despair.
Let the radiance of mercy
rest on your forehead and let your words
be as diamonds of love,
falling like rain,
nurturing and transforming all they touch.
I make your soul rich
in My kingdom,
for in Me there is no lack
and My riches are from everlasting
to everlasting—
I am greater than what you own
or don't own.
See yourself rising up tall,
rich in the glory
of My unlimited resources.

Psalm 45:13; 63:5; James 5:11; Isaiah 11:2; 58:11; John 6:63; Matthew 5:6; 5:13; Revelation 7:16

The Minister

The LORD will guide you always;
he will satisfy your needs in a sun-scorched land
and will strengthen your frame.
You will be like a well-watered garden,
like a spring whose waters never fail.

ISAIAH 58:11 NIV

Your hand, dearest one—
I reach for your precious hand.
Yes, give it to Me.
You've chosen to help those
who are hurting and oppressed,
and I have gone before you in
your task. See how I love
those I've sent you to.
I am in you as you share
your bread with the hungry,
as you help the helpless, clothe the naked,
and spread My Word.
I want to free oppressed souls,
shatter bonds of wickedness,

and break the yokes that enslave My children,
and I do this by My Spirit
in you.
Because you love Me with your whole heart
and continually raise your voice in worship,
My Presence goes before you.
I promise you that the damaged
and wounded places of your life
will hinder you no more.
You will blossom like a fertile plain
as My empowering gifts burgeon in you,
as you choose to be strong
and not weak, going forth
surrendered to Me. I alone lead you,
and you will flourish as a watered garden,
a crystal spring whose shower never runs dry.
You will rebuild the bedlam
and be called the repairer of the breach.
You will delight in Me as you work,
and I will delight in you, for
out of My burning passion
I have made you a flame of fire.

Psalm 101:1–3; Isaiah 58:1–2; 11–12; Psalm 104:4; Hebrews 1:7; Psalm 103:21b

Bless the Lord

Bless—affectionately, gratefully praise—
the Lord, O my soul, and all that is
[deepest] within me, bless His holy name!

Psalm 103:1 AMP

When you command your soul to bless the Lord,
to affectionately and gratefully praise Me
with all that is deepest within you,
My many benefits are unleashed to you
in waves of love.
Your life is redeemed from the pit of corruption
and defeat. You are beautified, dignified,
and crowned with loving-kindness and My most
tender mercies.
Your necessities are met,
your youth is renewed, the desires
of your heart are met.
I heal your body and infuse you with zeal
and purpose.
Roll your works upon Me, trust Me wholly.
My Holy Spirit gives you revelation into My Word

and recognition of My blessings.
To you it is given to know the mystery
of the kingdom of God
because you insist upon a life
vitally united to Me. By choosing to live
solely in and for Me and by commanding your soul
to bless the Lord,
you enter into My innermost chambers,
where you are guided into all truth.
Your gift to Me and your world
is to walk as I would walk.
I am in your shoes.

Psalm 103:1–5; Mark 4:11; John 15:7; 16:13;
Galatians 5:16, 25

Lord, I'm Surrounded by Problems

You, through Your commandments,
make me wiser than my
enemies. . . .

Psalm 119:98 NKJV

Lord, I'm surrounded
by problems and turmoil.
All I see are
problems and misery
and sin.
I'm afraid these
are going to
rub off on me.
Help.

I'm here.
I am with you
and within you to give you
supernatural ability
and control.
Don't conform
to the disenchantment of the world
nor allow its fears and habits
to snatch your peace.
Remove yourself!
My Holy Spirit
transforms you daily
with love and power
to raise you to a place of
strength and dignity.
Separate yourself.
Prove for yourself
what My good and acceptable
and perfect will is for you.
I will renew your mind constantly
and keep you pure,
but you must surround yourself
with Me, My Word, and
fellowship with other believers.

Keep yourself from being
stained by the world.
MOVE ON,
I say.

Jeremiah 31:3; Romans 12:2; 2 Corinthians 6:17

The Deceiver

Be sober, be vigilant; because your adversary
the devil walks about
like a roaring lion,
seeking whom he may devour.

1 Peter 5:8 NKJV

You are Mine. Your enemy knows that
and he trembles.
 Put aside naïve interpretations of who I am
 and what I do, and trust in My written Word.
The devil will steal
anything he can get from you.
 In cunning hatred
 he claws, chews, lies, roars,
 and assaults in order to kill.
He is capable of making you believe ugly is
beautiful.
 He will try to convince you that
 your self-indulgence is good.
Do not be a plaything for this liar
and cunning deceiver.

Be trained by My Spirit for battle,
disciplined in your affections.
Don't mistake evil for good.
I give you a heavenly appetite. I give you holy eyes
to see truth and a mind to flourish with the beauty of God.
I give you an invitation to an open heaven.
I put My words in your mouth
and cover you with the shadow of My hand.
I teach you the paths of wisdom.
I give you insight into My ways
and visions of My kingdom in glory.
You cannot be defeated.

---

1 Peter 5:9; 2 Corinthians 2:11; James 2:19; Proverbs 4:11; 1 Corinthians 16:13; Psalm 125:1

Ending Your War With Others

A soft answer turns away wrath.

Proverbs 15:1a NKJV

Don't be surprised when a child of Mine
offends you, for it's bound to happen.
They may roil with jealousy or contention
because I have shown you favor.
They may not approve of your ways
or your ministry. They may backbite,
or kindle fires with rumors and untruths
that scorch and wound. Do not strike back.
Don't take an eye for an eye. If your brother
or sister strikes you a blow on the cheek,
turn your face for more. It is a fool
who is eager to quarrel.
Indeed, you've initiated foolish battles
that should not have been fought.
You jumped forward swinging both fists at
the mere whisper of opposition.

Be slow to retaliate, dear one. Show your depth
of spiritual wisdom, and don't exalt the flesh.
Your brother and sister are not your enemies.
The enemy is the devil. He stalks around
looking for someone willing to pick a fight,
someone
like you, whose feelings are easily injured.
Your kind and gentle heart is replaced
with angry self-defense,
and you're no longer fit for the Master's use.
If you wage war against a brother or sister,
whom shall I send to protect them against *you*?
Readily pardon, even as I freely pardon you.
Wash your hands and purify your heart;
consider those who hurt, malign,
and offend you as better than yourself.
At the root of every unmerited rebuke
and curse,
I am there. The curse without a cause can't
touch you.
I want you trained by My spirit, refined
in every aspect, able to find a star
in the blackest night,

treasure in the midst of scorn, joy in spite of rejection,

and peace in the center of My love.

Proverbs 4:13–15; 14:29, 33; Exodus 14:14; 1 John 1:7; 4:7; Philippians 2:3

Through the Fire

We went through fire and water, but you brought us to a place of abundance.

Psalm 66:12b NIV

The scourging flames
twist and scatter
against the walls of your sunrise
like tortured rags;
scalding sparks shoot in every direction,
turning to smoldering cinder
all they light upon.
You stand in the midst of the furnace
of flames,
thirsty,
hot,
nervous.
Will the fire char and turn you to ash,
or will it form you into
a messenger of truth?

Will you pass
through the blazing inferno without
fear, singing My praises,
wearing the boots of faith?
Will you conquer the fang-toothed
demons of terror who thrill to cast their
screaming flames at you?
Dear one,
the way to victory
is to wield the sword of the Spirit and
march right on through the flames.
Do it.

1 Corinthians 3:13; Malachi 3:2–3; 1 Peter 1:7; Isaiah 43:2;
Daniel 3:25–27

The Golden Orb of My Promises

Therefore know that the LORD your God, He is God,
the faithful God who keeps covenant and mercy
for a thousand generations with those who love Him
and keep His commandments.

DEUTERONOMY 7:9

I have made many promises to you,
and it is not My will
that you forget them.
I tell you,
My Word to you is sure.
I AM My Word. When I answer
your cry to Me with a promise,
it is everlasting and true.
MY WORDS WILL COME TO PASS.
Have you forgotten the two immutable things
the Lord your God *cannot* do?
I cannot lie and I cannot break a covenant.

Hold fast your promise, I say. Remember
Sarah of old, who, though barren,
received My promise to conceive a child.
Did she not give birth to a son?
Did Hannah also not receive My promise
to bear a son? And Elizabeth?
And did My Father not promise His Son
to the world?
Though you feel forgotten in a desert
of thorns and dust,
I have not forgotten you.
You are ever before Me.

My promises to you
are as an orb of gold for you to press
into your heart. You are to sleep with this orb
of My promises so you wake to My promises
and walk in My promises all day long. Take your
power. Stand up and be strong.
You cannot be strong without patience
and humility. You cannot birth
greatness without trust. You cannot live
without faith. I tell you,

you are going to birth great treasures
for the kingdom of God.
Will you believe?

Hebrews 6:18; Titus 1:2; Numbers 23:19; 1 Samuel 15–20; Luke 1:11–23; John 3:16; 1 Kings 8:56; 2 Peter 1:4; Romans 8:17–18

When You Don't Know What to Say

The mind of the wise instructs his mouth, and adds learning and persuasiveness to his lips.

Proverbs 16:23 AMP

Do not be intimidated by human wisdom.
Do not hold back because you feel
your words will not be impressive.
I use the simple things of life as mighty.
I have chosen babes to influence kings.
I have chosen the weak to be strong.
I have chosen the foolish to confound the wise.
I create a new communication in you.
I create a new vocabulary in your mouth.
Once you belched words like smoke
and meaningless vapors,
but now you build victorious cities
with new words of life.
No longer do I hear you drip empty phrases
that dry up in the sun,

but you speak words as apples of gold.
When you rule your spirit, you speak
with discretion and wisdom,
deep as water,
plenteous and fathomless.
Your words are fed by My fountain
of skillful wisdom and are as a gushing stream—
sparkling, fresh, pure, and life-giving.
I give you the ability to bring
your heavenly Father
much pleasure by the radiant expressions
of His own mind. So allow the truth
I have taught you to permeate your words.
My heart will be glad and you will rejoice
when your lips speak the words I have taught you,
when your lips pour forth from
your heart's fountain of life.
Today allow Me to give you the tongue
of a disciple, the tongue of one who is taught by Me
in order that you always know how to speak
a word in season to someone weary
(including yourself)—in order that you will know
how to speak to Me.

I wake you morning by morning
to hear My words and communicate
with Me.
And if you can hear My words,
you can speak them.
You know what to say.
Let Me hear you.

Proverbs 16:24; 18:4; Isaiah 50:4; 1 Corinthians 14:25;
1 Thessalonians 5:17

Reap What You Sow

Now this I say, he who sows sparingly shall also reap sparingly; and he who sows bountifully shall also reap bountifully.

2 CORINTHIANS 9:6 NASB

A bird in flight,
    a rabbit running,
a skittering insect.
    Behold, all of life
moves.
    Leaves in trees bristle
and flutter,
    then float downward
to the earth. The clouds
    jostle the landscape of the sky,
and the wind moves as
    restless fringe across the earth.
All that lives moves.

Even the smallest cell
throbs,
pulses,
breathes.

But fear will paralyze you,
turn your bones stiff,
and your breath stale.
You remain inert and fret—
should you turn left or right?
What matters is that you *turn*.
You want to know which color to use
on your canvas;
what matters is that you *choose*.
Birds build nests in your worries.
Fret and worry
bring Me no pleasure.
Do not shrink back. I can't guide you
if you are not moving.
Move, I say!
Be bold!
Do you wish you could see into
the portals of tomorrow
to be positively sure you'll succeed?
These concerns are vain, futile.

Your prayers will form
stagnant lakes in your head.
Your feet will be buried in weeds,
your dreams will wander like smoke.
You gain only as you give.
Wake up!
No energy spent in My kingdom
is wasted.

Invest in the kingdom of God
for a holy return.
Don't stand still.
No time is ever lost in a labor of love
for Me. My rewards are not like the rewards
of the world, not flattering,
nor temporary.
I bless the soul. I enrich the heart.
I kiss the spirit.

Hebrews 10:38; Job 12:10; Acts 17:28; Matthew 10:31;
2 John 8; 1 Timothy 5:6; Luke 6:38; Hebrews 11:6;
1 Corinthians 15:58; John 15:9

Because I Am a Giving God

Yes, the LORD will give what is good.

PSALM 85:12A NKJV

Because I am a giving God and I love you,
I give wisdom and knowledge and joy
to you, My child, who pleases Me!
Because I am a giving God, and I love you,
I bring you to a place of great delight.
I meet all your needs.
I keep you safe and blessed
in a place where you lack no good thing.

Because I am a giving God and I love you,
I gladly give you the secret knowledge
of the mysteries of the kingdom of heaven.
And because you choose My Spirit,
and a life in Me,
more will be given to you.

I am a giving God and I love you.
Even if you see yourself as a small sparrow
alone on a housetop, know that I see you.
I am there with you
because I am a giving God and I love you.

And if you are lauded as the star of a million parades
with your laurels marching before you, and
if your name commands the applause of throngs,
and if you sleep in the beds of kings,
ride the wings of skillful knowledge in all things,
I am there.
I am a giving God and I love you.
If you feel abandoned by every soul you ever trusted
and your days are laced in tears,
I am there.
I am a giving God and I love you.

I tell you, you can conquer impossible worlds
when you wield the powerful sword of
My Word
with the mighty banner of faith. You will
accomplish great feats in My name,
greater than you have
asked Me for. Oh, fly the heights
and scour the depths spread out
before you with your arms outstretched and
following My lead.
Greet every dawn with trembling
expectation!
Celebrate the sunrise and the sunset.
I am in the morning light
and in the evening dusk.
I tell you, I am there!
I am there in sunlight and in shadows.
I am there in hunger and in fatness,
in your youth and in your old age.
I stick to you like your own skin.
The mountains of the earth
will shake and crumble,

but My tender love for you is never
shaken—
not a shiver,
not a breath,
not the barest vibration or change
because I am a giving God
and I love you.

Ecclesiastes 2:26; Deuteronomy 8:7–9; Philippians 4:19;
Matthew 13:11–13, 23; Psalm 139:9–10; Proverbs 18:24

Forever Pardoned

Therefore, if anyone is in Christ, he is a new creation;
old things have passed away; behold,
all things have become new.

2 Corinthians 5:17 NKJV

And as I forgive you,
dear one,
so you ought also
to forgive yourself.
It is good to deny yourself
the absurdity of a self-centered life
and recognize your efforts to accomplish
your dreams are futile without Me in control.
To be dead to sin and selfishness
means to live at last—
to climb out of the mire
of mistakes and loss. It means to live clean
and beautiful with eyes no longer blinded
and a heart no longer made of stone.
Only then can you walk in forgiveness,
forgiving yourself and all

who have sinned against you.
Attainments, accolades, awards, and prizes
pass away, and yesterday's crimes
and failures dry up as mud in the glory
of forgiveness.
Your rewards lie far beyond
what you have tried to accomplish
in your own strength.
When you are one with Me,
our achievements dance around us
like jeweled children.
I forgive,
I restore,
I make new.
Your pardon is forever. All is well.

Hebrews 10:22; Philippians 4:7; Micah 7:18; Isaiah 51:11

THE GIFT OF SIMPLICITY

At that time Jesus answered and said, "I thank You, Father, Lord of heaven and earth, that You have hidden these things from the wise and prudent and have revealed them to babes."

MATTHEW 11:25 NKJV

My Son came to you holy,
innocent, undefiled,
unstained by sin,
and it is His cross you carry,
His life you lead,
His words you've learned to cherish.
Seek My kingdom first
and you shall have
all that the heart requires.
Simplicity discerns what is evil with a single eye,
and in the joyful sweetness of this wisdom,
you choose only what glorifies your God.
I reside at the center of this glory,
where there is no fragmentation;
I transcend both fear and human reason.

I am the core and substance of life,
where there is nothing so complex to
jar one breath of My kingdom on earth.
I illuminate the galaxies and all the heavens,
and you possess the personality of this light
in your simplicity.
You wear the cloak of divine approval,
and therefore it is needful you resist
the urge to join the throngs of others who
busy themselves pursuing currents of
cultural trends.
The silly and seducible ones
chase after the lower concerns of the soul
and are met with guile and shame, but
My simple babe in power, might, and wisdom
pursues the higher things and sees God.

Hebrews 7:26; Matthew 10:16; 6:25, 33

The Gift of Laughter

"Blessed are you who weep now,
for you shall laugh."
LUKE 6:21 NASB

Laughter does not exclude weeping.
When pain and hardship confront you
and the scars of oppression line your face,
I will remove the sting of defeat
and the stab of failure
and loss.
Joy is no stranger to pain.
When you go out from your interior pain
weeping, but carrying seeds of hope
to plant in spiritually barren deserts,
you will return one day
accompanied by holy laughter.
Joy calls your name,
pursues you.
The walls of heaven are assembled
in such joy, their voice goes out continually

on the wings of the wind.
Holy laughter surrounds you because
you are confident in Me.
You rise up to toss your head and laugh
at trials and troubles
in praise and holy wonder.
Laughter is the child
of trust, beloved—
My gift to you.
You have learned
the private language of heaven.

Luke 6:21; Nehemiah 8:10; Psalm 126:5–6; Luke 6:21;
Psalm 30:11; Job 8:21

The Language of a Thankful Heart

Enter into His gates
with thanksgiving,
And into His courts with praise.
Be thankful to Him,
and bless His name.

PSALM 100:4 NKJV

Cherish thankfulness. Know that even now
you are partaking of the same joyous experience
of angels who surround the throne of God
giving thanks to the Lord God almighty,
who is and was and will come!
Let thankfulness, My dearest child, constantly
and at all times, gush upward to Me
from your heart and your mouth.
In all circumstances, let the treasure
of your thankful heart rule your spirit.

The language of a thankful heart
is the language of glory, for the quality of praise
transcends all things base and earthly.

Lean your entire personality on Me
and give thanks. See how strong
your heart becomes,
and how, in an oppressed and thankless world,
the beautiful light of your life radiates
with favor.

1 Thessalonians 5:18; Hebrews 13:15; Genesis 28:15; Deuteronomy 31:6; Joshua 1:5; Colossians 1:9–12, 14; Proverbs 12:2

THE GIFT OF RESTORATION

And in that day you will say:
"O LORD, I will praise You;
Though You were angry with me,
Your anger is turned away, and
You comfort me."

ISAIAH 12:1 NKJV

I am calling to the heart of you
to tell you that your warfare
will end
and your iniquity be removed.
I comfort you.
For though you have polluted your calling
and sinned against My love for you,
I am calling you now
to clear a trail through the hollows
of your life and
make a smooth path from your heart
to your mind

that I might return
    and take residence upon the throne
    of your soul
once more.

Isaiah 40:1–3

The Gift of the Cross

And being found in appearance as a man,
He humbled Himself
and became obedient to the point of death,
even the death of the cross.

PHILIPPIANS 2:8 NKJV

I want to open the eyes of your understanding
so you can see yourself
as you really are.
When you came to Me,
your sins, sensuality, and carnal nature
had you fastened to a death course
like a fly caught in a spider's web—
making noise, but stuck.
Dust has no life of its own,
but just one breath from Me
and dust became a human race.
And today because you are Mine,
I lift you up and set you free
to be all that I created you to be—
your real self.

Your carnal nature with its shady passions
    and lusts are stripped from you
and nailed to the cross of My Son Jesus.

When I created you, I had in mind a *friend.*
    The path to My friendship
is by way of the cross of Christ,
    where your old life is buried
because My Son did the dying for you.
    When you fear the influence of sin
coming against you, don't look at *you,*
    look to the cross!
There you will see yourself as you really are—
    altogether new in Christ, crucified with Him,
living through Him,
    and daily renewed and remolded after the image
and likeness of Me.

---

1 Corinthians 1:17–18; Genesis 2:7; Colossians 2:11–15; 3:10; Galatians 2:20; Hebrews 1:3; Romans 8:29

THE GIFT OF ARMOR

Put on the full armor of God, that you may
be able to stand firm against the schemes of the devil.

EPHESIANS 6:11 NASB

Your worst temptation may be
attempting to resist sin
without your spiritual armor.
Your enemy, the devil, entices you,
and stirs your old nature into action,
and if you try to resist sin with
your soul's strategies, you will fail.
Self-will can never conquer
mighty spiritual controls.
The real enemies of humankind are not
other humans, but powers and master spirits
who are world rulers and
spirit forces of wickedness.

My holy armor is a shield
of incorruptible faith in Me, and you
are strong in Me and in the power
of *My* might.
Only wearing your spiritual armor
can you vanquish a spiritual foe.
Take My written Word as your
mighty sword and shred to bits every snare
of the enemy.
Stand firm, unafraid as a conqueror,
for defeat is not caused by less effort
on your part,
but by too much effort
without protection.

Ephesians 6:10–17

I Love to Do Good for You

I will rejoice in doing them good
and will assuredly plant them in this land
with all my heart and soul.
Jeremiah 32:41 NIV

To be one with you like this,
My child,
to hear words of praise
from so true a heart,
to know these glowing moments
when you and I
are loving, captivated, engaged in perfect
communion—
this is the purpose of My Son's death
on the cross.
He is the link between us,
He who opened heaven's walls
to let you enter in.
Take in My Word:

Taste, eat, see, and know
the heart and mind of God.
I am the One
who formed you,
and breathes breath into your nostrils.
I love to accomplish good for you.
I give you opportunities like shining halos;
take them and be blessed with good.
I also give you challenges,
unleashed from a sanctuary of bees.
Meet them without fear
because you wear divine protection.
I give you the opportunity to know Me
and to bless Me,
and this is good.
Take the opportunity now
to bring to Me,
like delicacies on a platter,
the joy
the angels love to see,
the joy you were born
to experience.
Come now,
let Me hold you near
and give you good.

Come now, beloved,
  let me kiss your heart
and give you My best.

John 15:4; Psalm 31:19; Nehemiah 8:10; Jeremiah 23:23

THE GLORY OF YOU

For me, to live is Christ.
PHILIPPIANS 1:21A NASB

For indeed, the kingdom of God is within you.
LUKE 17:21B NKJV

Allow My Word to pulsate
with urgency
in the core of your being, and
My Presence will saturate all
of you.
Dear one, I hold and maintain all
that concerns you.
I am ever at your right hand.
Let your heart be glad and your spirit
rejoice. Let your body
be a buttress of confidence. I direct
and lay before you the path of
a higher life,
with exquisite joy and peace.

In My right hand are pleasures
to thrive forevermore.
Allow My Spirit
to become the Source of all your activity.
The kingdom of God is at hand!
Possess Me and you possess My kingdom.
Be consumed with loving Me.
I am your everything.
This is your glory.

1 Peter 4:2, 6; Psalm 16:5–11; Luke 17:21; Colossians 2:10

Lord, I'm a Perfectionist

His divine power has given us
everything we need for life and godliness
through our knowledge of him
who called us by his own glory and goodness.

2 Peter 1:3 NIV

Lord, I always thought
doing things perfectly
was the only acceptable way.
I do everything to the very best
of my ability, and isn't that
what you ask?
I like a job well done,
I like orderliness and neatness.
I like winning. Is this wrong?
I'm never truly happy because
things are never as perfect as I

want them to be. Help me improve.
Help me be more perfect.

Oh, dear one! I don't ask you to be Me,
only to be like Me.
If you are like Me,
you are gentle, kind, patient;
you are tenderhearted, honest,
and your motives are pure.
You are filled with My Spirit and
your desire is to know and love Me.
Led by My Spirit, you are not
driven by vain and crushing demands
for excellence.
Search your heart, beloved.
Your stressful ways
are more damaging than you know.
Being plagued with ungodly drives
to achieve mutes the soft voice
of My Spirit calling you,
guiding you,
loving you.
I alone can satisfy the longing soul.

For what does your soul long?
I do not promise you perfection,
I promise you greatness.

Romans 8:29; 1 John 4:16; Luke 10:40–42; Psalm 107:9;
2 Corinthians 9:8; Matthew 20:26

My Showcase

And the glory which You gave Me I have given them,
that they may be one just as We are one.

John 17:22 NKJV

Let your spirit live
in a greater consciousness of My will.
Let My will cohabit your will
like a penetrating light,
giving you clear vision on all sides.
When your will becomes one with Mine,
I prepare your mind with truth
concerning all events of life.
Daily training in My Spirit's vision
gives you eyes to see
as I see, ears to hear as I hear,
a mind to discern as I do.
You have been created by Me
to go forth into life
with great openness of heart—
to pray without ceasing,

to love as I love.
    The saint of God must know
    when to fight
    and when to be still.
I will make you rise up, furious as a lion,
    and leap upon the enemy
in My name.
    My Spirit will accomplish this.
I love to look upon your face and love you,
    I love to listen to your adoring heart.
You have found Me
    and found your life.
Love Me.
Worship Me.
Talk to Me.
Listen to Me.

Find your life exciting, let your soul delight itself
    in My abundant blessings,
because you, beloved,
    are My showcase.

Ecclesiastes 3:5; Zechariah 10:5; 1 Thessalonians 5:17; Psalm 17:15; Proverbs 4:13; Romans 9:21; 1 Peter 5:4; John 12:26; 17:22; 1 John 4:7–8; Isaiah 55:2b; 2 Corinthians 4:17

When You Cry

You number my wanderings;
Put my tears into Your bottle;
Are they not in Your book?

Psalm 56:8 NKJV

Nothing escapes My attention,
beloved. Each hair of your head
is important enough for Me
to keep count of. I rescue you
and I continue to rescue you.
Shall I gather your tears
from the bottles you've filled for Me and
draw forth an ocean of them?
Shall I give a name to this great, sad body
of bitter waters?
Shall we call it simply *yours*?
But then it will remain as yours, your own
private ocean of tears. Dear one, I have promised
weeping shall endure only for a night.
Though the dark night hours be long and painful,
I've promised joy at the morning light.

I'll make your tears a crown and a blessing,
    awash with the fresh promise of
a luminous new day.
    All soul-bound shrines to pain
    will come to nothing, no matter how sad.
I know what to do with your tears.
    When you give your tears to Me, they are
no longer yours.

Psalm 6:6; 30:5; Isaiah 25:8; Psalm 116:8; 56:8

NOTICED IN THE WORLD

"Do not fear, for I am with you;
Do not anxiously look
about you,
for I am your God.
I will strengthen you, surely I will
help you, surely I will uphold you
with My righteous right hand."

ISAIAH 41:10 NASB

Stop saying you have no power.
Be as the prophet who said,
"As for me,
I am filled with power,
with the Spirit of the Lord,
and with justice and might."

If you bear the name Christian,
you cannot walk in the world unnoticed.

I have armed you with strength,
it never runs out.
You are one who can soar
on wings like eagles,
you can run and not grow weary,
you can walk and not be faint.
Do nothing out of fear.
Never be dismayed.
I am your God.
Fear is not your God.

I pamper your soul,
but not your fear.
I answer every prayer,
but I do not spoil you
by catering to your old nature.
Never be overcome with inadequacy.
No one led by My Spirit is inadequate
for the tasks I dispense.

Micah 3:8; Isaiah 40:31; 41:10; Ephesians 3:16–17;
Zechariah 4:6

God's Omnipresence

"Am I a God who is near," declares the Lord, *"and not a God far off? Can a man hide himself in hiding places, so I do not see him?" declares the* Lord. *"Do I not fill the heavens and the earth?" declares the* Lord.

Jeremiah 23:23–24 NASB

I have searched you and known you,
I know when you sit down and when you rise up,
I understand your thoughts from any distance,
I scrutinize the choices you make,
and I am with you
when you lie down to sleep.
I am intimately acquainted with all your ways.
Even before you utter a word, I know it.
I have enclosed you with My protection
and love
from before and behind.
My hand is upon you always.

So I ask you:
Where can you go from My Spirit?
Where can you run from My presence?
If you try to scale a ladder to heaven,
I am there;
If you climb upon the wings of the morning
on an early flight to the ends of the earth,
or if you book passage on a ship and live in its belly
in the center of the sea,
My eye is there.

O dearest one, with storm-tossed thoughts,
think on this:
My mind is in your mind.
My spirit is over your spirit.
My *self* is in your self.
My presence is in your presence.
For I saw you before you could be seen,
and I wrote about you
when there was nothing to write about.
My thoughts of you outnumber the sands.

The speed of light cannot outrun Me,
darkness and light are alike to Me.

Neither by night nor day
can you escape My heart.
I am here to help you.
My right hand protects you,
holds you close.
You cannot be unloved.

Psalm 139

HAPPY AND CONTENTED

You will be happy and
it will be well with you.
PSALM 128:2B NASB

Come away with Me, My beloved!
    Let us laugh and be free,
let us rest and be glad
    and enjoy the sounds of contentment.
What pleasure we can share!
    I love not only your labor
    that you do in My name,
        I also love your recreation.

Take pleasure, dearest,
when you play—as unto Me,
    and play with all your heart!
Your confident bearing
    will be a blessing
    to all who play with you.

I am with you, too, for I never leave you
or forsake you.
    When you are in need of rest,
    I offer you spiritual refreshment,
    physical and mental relief
    in recreation.
Be light and keep your humor,
    sharpen your wit,
put on your athletic prowess,
    relax and enjoy.
And keep Me with you,
    because I delight
    in all of you.

1 Timothy 6:6; Hebrews 4:3; Exodus 33:14; Hebrews 13:5;
Matthew 11:28; Proverbs 12:22; Isaiah 62:4

Helping Is Good

Bear one another's burdens, and so fulfill the law of Christ.
For if anyone thinks himself to be something,
when he is nothing, he deceives himself.

GALATIANS 6:2–3 NKJV

How heavy is your burden?
Can you, beneath the weight
of your own burden,
lighten the burden of someone else?
When you complain that the veil of trouble
is too thick around you,
that you cannot feel My loving-kindness;
when you bemoan
that you can't do anything right—
how can you help anyone else?
You are never so helpless that
you cannot give help.
You are never too lame
to lift up another,
never too blind

to help another find the proper path,
never too groggy of mind
to reach out your hand to one
in need,
speaking My love
even without words.
What does your life mean
to you?
What on earth can give you
the deep, satisfying delight
of doing the work
I do?
The greatest truth of life
is this
and always will be:
I am your life.

Jude 1:22–23; Acts 20:35; 1 Thessalonians 5:14; Psalm 41:1–3; Galatians 2:20

LORD, BLESS MY HUSBAND

Let each man have his own wife, and let each woman have her own husband. Let the husband fulfill his duty to his wife, and likewise also the wife to her husband.

1 CORINTHIANS 7:2–3 NASB

Help me to love my husband, Lord,
to cherish him
the way he deserves
to be cherished.

A wise and intelligent wife is
a gift from Me,
and your husband has found
that which is
true and good. I chose him for you.
You are more precious
than jewels;

your value exceeds that
of rubies or pearls.
I have called a woman to be earnest
and strong in character,
virtuous, wise, and capable.
When she marries
she is a crowning joy to her husband,
and it is with great delight
that a man can trust and rely on his wife
with confidence.
She will comfort, encourage,
and do him good
all the days of her life.
Your husband is your friend
and your lover,
and I will guide and help him
to love and bless you,
and to treat you
as I treat you—
for I love you
with a perfect love.
I give you My special blessing
and ability to love your husband
as you love Me,
for he is worthy of your love.

In your union
of harmony and mutual respect,
as joint-heirs and partners
in the kingdom of God,
I am glorified.

Proverbs 19:14; 31:10; 12:4; 31:11–12; 1 Corinthians 7:3; Ephesians 5:2, 24

Lord, Bless My Wife

So husbands ought also to love their own wives
as their own bodies.
He who loves his own wife
loves himself.

EPHESIANS 5:28 NASB

Father, thank You for my wife.
Help me to be the kind of husband
You want me to be
and to love my wife
as You love her.

The calling of a husband
is a high calling.
As Christ is the husband
of all believers
(in the church, the bride of Christ),
so you are the husband
of the woman
I have given you.

Love her,
honor her,
and listen to her.
Nurture your friendship,
for she will be
a foundation of strength for you
and a faithful voice of encouragement.
Your marriage will be
unshaken by the storms
of life.
Love her as you love yourself,
let her grow and bloom
as I lead her,
and never quench My Spirit
in her.
Together you are a mighty team,
a joy to heaven,
and a delight to Me.

Proverbs 18:22; Ephesians 5:25, 28; Psalm 149:4;
1 Corinthians 7:3; Proverbs 5:18–19; Luke 12:32

Never Too Late

My times are in Your hand.
PSALM 31:15A NKJV

Never judge your life by the limitations of time:
The Lord Jesus was thirty years old
before entering His public ministry,
and He ministered but three short years.
When He died on the cross
there were still millions of souls
who remained unreached,
untaught,
unhealed.
But in His holy obedience and love
He glorified Me perfectly
and fulfilled My will.
I do not live in time.
Time does not limit Me.
A moment is as a thousand years
in My economy. Your task is to discover and
complete

My will for you no matter how long
or short a time it involves.
My Son was unrestrained by
the boundaries of time,
and was, therefore, never anxious,
never rushed, and never stressed.
Fix your goals of excellence
on your spiritual calling,
and never on *time,*
for I instruct and teach you in the way
you shall go, I guide you with My eyes
ever upon you.
Your life is to fulfill My will.
This is the ecstasy and the promise
we share.

Psalm 143:10; Philippians 2:8; Matthew 26:42; Psalm 32:8;
Philippians 1:9–11

END THE WAR WITH YOURSELF

And, beloved, if our consciences (our hearts) do not accuse us—if they do not make us feel guilty and condemn us—we have confidence (complete assurance and boldness) before God.

1 JOHN 3:21 AMP

How often I've called you in love and affection.
How often I've sung over you in the night watches
and held you safe in My arms as the arrows
of the day assailed you.
Yet, as I sing over you I hear another voice.
What is that sound? Is it the voice of your
self-contempt? Is it you cursing your life
in a private battle cry
against yourself?—Against the one I love?
I want you to speak of yourself
as though it was I, the Father,
describing you. The new life I give you
makes no room for self derision.

You are My own handiwork, My workmanship,
recreated in Christ Jesus, born anew so you may
do the good works
I have prepared for you and to
fulfill your destiny in Me.
Be careful with your mouth before uttering
those negative, demeaning words
about My precious child.
I am the forgiver of all the mistakes and sins
you will ever commit
just for the asking. When you
confess and turn from your sins, I do
a royal clean-up in your life.
To speak kindly of yourself is to humble yourself.
To hold yourself in esteem is to humble yourself.
To be gentle with yourself is to hold Me
in esteem.

Because you love Me,
shake yourself from the dust,
loose yourself from the bonds
around your neck
and enjoy being a child of My heart.
End the war with yourself.

Romans 8:1, 31–39; Proverbs 19:8; Ecclesiastes 5:2; 2:10; Jeremiah 31:3

Take Your Authority in Me

Commit your way to the LORD,
Trust also in Him,
And He shall bring it to pass.
He shall bring forth your
righteousness as the light,
And your justice as the noonday.

PSALM 37:5–6 NKJV

The justice you crave is Mine.
I want to show you how to stand
for what is yours.
I want you to use your authority in Me
and come into my holy courtroom with your case.
Come, let us reason together.
You are Mine, and your life is ever before Me.
When you are accused and tempted by the enemy,
who is your defender? your advocate?
I make Myself known in the flames of judgment,
I sit on My throne and maintain your rights

and your cause as My child
because you are washed completely clean
in the blood of My Son, Jesus.
Your enemies are not flesh and blood, and
I tell you, you are no longer to present yourself
as fodder for the demons of hell
to render you stupid to their wiles.
You are vindicated by God!
Jesus, My Son, paid the penalty for your freedom
from all enemy schemes. Take your authority
and stand fast in your liberty from the tangles
of bondage. I have removed the chains
that once held you in defeat and failure. Stand,
therefore, I say, stand in the power
of My might. No word or act of condemnation
will succeed
against My righteous ones
in My court. I want you to be
strong
and live your life as a miracle of freedom.

Isaiah 1:18; 1 John 2:1; Psalm 9:4, 16; Luke 18:7;
Ephesians 6:12; Galatians 5:1; 1 Timothy 3:16; Romans 8:30

Beyond the Gates of Grace

It is vain for you to rise up early,
to take rest late, to eat the bread of [anxious] toil;
for He gives [blessings] to His beloved in sleep.

PSALM 127:2 AMP

I never sulk, but you are sulking.
I never pout, but you are pouting.
I never complain, or shrink back in fear.
But look at you.
I created you and formed you in My image
to draw you into My heart
and share not only My likeness
but also My thoughts.
You were created
to reflect the Father's personality
and to please Him.
Have you pressed yourself behind the gates of grace?
Have you looked for *signs* of Me
instead of Me?

Where do you run for personal safety?
Under the table,
behind the bed,
or to My heavenly high tower?
Where do you run for help in time of want?
To the pharmacy,
the supermarket,
or to My mercy, which lasts forever?
Where do you run for the miracle you need?
To the telephone,
to the newspaper,
or to your Savior, who promises to give what you ask for?
Do you seek Me in places I am not?
My desire is that you make your home in heavenly fields of gold,
above the cares and deceptions of the world,
not in the mud below.

Isaiah 40:28–31; Nehemiah 8:10; Ephesians 1:19–23;
Colossians 3:1–2; Isaiah 53:6; Psalm 59:9, 16–17

YOUR PRECIOUS FRAGRANCE

I will refresh Israel like the dew from heaven; she will blossom as the lily and root deeply in the soil like cedars in Lebanon. Her branches will spread out as beautiful as olive trees, fragrant as the forests of Lebanon.

HOSEA 14:5–6 TLB

Your love for Me
  is a beautiful fragrance, not only reaching Me,
but touching your world
  like the scent of cedar, savory and refreshing.
The perfume of My presence is what you bring
to the created world when you love Me. I am with all
  who love Me.

Your love for Me is more pleasing than the scent
  of the lily in the earth.

Your love for Me brings Me pleasure.

As you present yourself to Me in love,

I meet you. And I meet all your needs
according to My riches in glory.

Your unselfish gifts shared in love become

a sweet fragrance to Me. Your words of love
drip sweetness as the honeycomb.

My Holy Spirit will continually refresh you
like dew from heaven.

I perfume your spirit.

Your personal fragrance
is spawned in the attitudes of your heart.

Your fragrance is your message.

Philippians 4:18–19; 2 Corinthians 2:15; Hosea 14:7;
Song of Solomon 6:2; 7:8; 4:10

Lord, to Be Closer to You

Your hands have made me and
fashioned me;
Give me understanding that I may
learn Your commandments.
Psalm 119:73 NKJV

Lord,
I don't know how to study
the Bible. I feel lost at sea
when it comes to learning
the Word and knowing You.

Lost? You are not lost
if you are Mine. You are a babe
in Me, my love, and you will grow.
Never fear.
You learn of Me by studying
to show yourself approved

with anointed teachers
of My Word, because faith
comes by hearing and hearing comes
by My Word taught soundly.
As you come to know Me,
your life changes and you
become more like Me.
And close to Me,
you won't want to leave
the most beautiful place
a human being can experience—
the interior of My heart.
I understand your bewildered state.
That is why you must keep your ears open
to learning, to becoming one
with My church, where My Word
goes forth.
Without teaching, the sounds of the world
will drown out My gentle urging,
and you will feel alone
and separated from Me.
But when you stay close to Me,
growing daily in My Word,
living in the blazing center

of My heart, dominated
and filled by the power of My Spirit,
you will know Me, and we will
become one.

1 John 2:15–17; 3:1–3; Romans 8:14; John 14:17

When You Feel the Chains of Guilt Around You

I have blotted out as a thick cloud your transgressions, and as a cloud your sins. Return to Me, for I have redeemed you.

Isaiah 44:22 AMP

You tend to see yourself as unclean, far removed from all that is heavenly.

I see you as My beloved.

You tend to see yourself as a hopeless backslider, a poor refugee scraping at the walls of the Promised Land.

I see you as Mine.

You can never dig too deep a hole for Me to pull you out. You can never take on the enemy's desperate lifestyle so wholly that I can't find you in sin's tangled briar and weeds.

You have grumbled that My ways are too hard, too prickly, too demanding. Do you think the tricks

of the prince of evil
are good to you? You trip blindly into his pit,
thinking you'll find roses there,
and then you howl
when you break your bones and
your possessions. You shake your fist at Me
as though I am the thief
you've consorted with.
Oh, afflicted one, storm-tossed
and not comforted,
I want to give you
a strong foundation.
I want to give you the life
I've ordained for you,
a life of victory and joy. When the corrupt
and malevolent
forsakes his way and relinquishes profane thoughts
and returns
to Me, I will love and have mercy on that one.
Hear Me in the wrestling of your mind,
for My call of love
is true and munificent. I am generous
with forgiveness,
and I love to multiply blessings upon My children.

I shall position you above oppression
and destruction.
I shall lift you up above guilt and shame.
Sin shall no longer be your master.
Don't caress guilt as though you own it.
Self-imposed guilt is like a curse,
but it must not remain
where it is not deserved. Confess to Me
your wandering soul, and the ease
with which you have blasphemed your Lord,
the One who loves you perfectly.
Feelings of guilt do not make you holy.
You have imagined there are sins I cannot
forgive.
Give up that thought.
Sacrifice and yield your thoughts to Me.
When you yield to Me,
I bathe your soul with the immaculate, perfect,
sinless blood of My Son,
which continues to gush from His veins for you.
his blood pours in constant healing and forgiving
to wash away all thoughts and acts contrary
to My will.

You can toss away your old tattered
and foul-smelling coat
of crusty shame and regrets
and put on your exquisite holy robe
of a new you
in Me.

Isaiah 55:7–9; 54:11, 14; 1 John 1:9; 2:12;
2 Corinthians 5:17; Ephesians 4:24

The Gift of Memory

"Thus says the Lord: 'I remember you.'"
Jeremiah 2:2 NKJV

I have inscribed you on the palms of My hands;
I will never forget you.
My promises to you are imprinted in My heart,
because My love for you
surpasses time and generations.

As the rainbow reminds the earth
of My solemn pledge
to hold back the floodwaters
from ever again swallowing the earth
and all its people, so I will remind you:
As you walk through the cities and nations
of the world in the furnaces of smoke
and consuming islands of fire,
you will not be afraid. You will expect great deeds
by My hand.

Remember the marvelous deeds I have done
and that I am LORD of all there is.
Remember you are Mine
and My Spirit is within you to work
the miracles you need.
I am the God of eternity and all creation.
Remember the signs and wonders
I have accomplished, and the ones
yet to come.
Remember My works and My love
from the foundation of the world.
Then build new memories,
new memories as My Spirit empowers you
to greater works.
Remember, and go forth.

Isaiah 49:16; Psalm 105:8; Genesis 19:29; Jonah 2:7;
Psalm 106:10, 14; John 14:12, 26; 2:23; Acts 2:42; Joel 2:28

The Gift of Multiplication

But also for this very reason, giving all diligence,
add to your faith virtue, to virtue knowledge,
to knowledge self-control, to self-control perseverance,
to perseverance godliness, to godliness brotherly kindness,
and to brotherly kindness love.
For if these things are yours and abound, you will be
neither barren nor unfruitful in the knowledge
of our Lord Jesus Christ.

2 Peter 1:5–8 NKJV

When you walk in obedience and surrender
to Me,
giving My Spirit permission to guide and permeate
all your decisions and actions,
My Spirit will multiply your gifts.
You can never be stagnant spiritually
when you live a Holy Spirit-controlled life.
My Spirit multiplies Myself in you.
I am Spirit.

Worship Me in spirit and in truth. Hear this instruction
    and be wise. Do not refuse
or neglect My words. Listen to Me
    and let Me multiply My power in you.
Allow Me to fill the treasuries of your desires.
    What I give you is better than
the world's choice silver and riches,
better than refined gold.
    Give your faith exercise, for faith
ignites itself and multiplies when exercised.
    As your faith multiplies, you will see miracles,
miracles kissed by My Spirit.
    Take wisdom as the builder of your house and
receive the favor of the Lord. Wisdom feeds you
    with the Bread of Life and gives you
its heavenly tonic to sip. You will be lifted to new
heights of understanding,
    and your faith is increased.
Your soul will delight itself in fatness.
    It is My desire to multiply Myself in you
    with My gifts and the fruits of My Spirit.
These will multiply in you and around you as you
    bow to My leading. Take more of My nature.

Take My compassion and kindness and let these
 multiply in you.
Take My forgiveness and mercy
 and let these multiply in you.
Take My power and My authority
 and let these multiply in you.
Let My glory and might
 be multiplied in the world
by My Spirit
 in you.

Mark 6:32–44; Ephesians 1:17–19; 2:10; Proverbs 9:1, 5–6; 8:19; 8:33; 8:35; 1 John 5:4; John 4:24; Hebrews 11:6; Matthew 17:20; Romans 10:17; 1 Corinthians 12:1–11; Galatians 5:16, 22–23

The Sounds of Joy

But let all those who take refuge and put
their trust in You, rejoice; let them ever sing,
and shout for joy, because You make a
covering over them and defend them;
let those also who love Your name be joyful
in You and be in high spirits.

Psalm 5:11 AMP

The sounds of joy
    are like the stretching of trees,
reaching upward
    to brush the floor of God.
The sounds of joy
    aspire higher than a human utterance,
resounding from one corner of the earth
    to the other,
so exhilarating
    it awakens that which lies in waste.
Joy startles the parched riverbeds,
    it stirs the dormant desert
and prods the dozing hills

awake to clap their hands
with the shout of the sea in its basin.
The sounds of joy
are like that of a host of the faithful
marching in triumph
to the house of the Lord—
even the rocks turn their faces
to the sun and sing along.
The sounds of joy
are like that of the mountains
shouting their mysteries across
the generations.
The sounds of joy
cry out as a voice in the wilderness,
exulting and proclaiming
the glory and majesty of God.
Let everything that has breath
and every trace of life
hear the sounds of joy,
for God dances in its corridors
and kisses the hearts of His children
who glory in His greatness.

Sing songs of triumph
with all that has a voice,
with the hail, the fog, and frost,
with storm and rain and drought,
for in the choruses of the wind
and within the swirling
heights and depths of the sounds of joy,
you will hear
the ravishing, omnipresent voice
of the heart of God.

Psalm 98:6, 8; 100:1; 150:1–6

Lord, I Thank You

I waited patiently for the LORD;
and He inclined to me,
And heard my cry.
He also brought me up out of a
horrible pit,
Out of the miry clay,
And set my feet upon a rock,
And established my steps.

PSALM 40:1–2 KJV

How can I thank You
for Your hand of love
on my life?
How can I thank You
for giving me back my health,
my strength,
my youth?
You have added to me
blessings and delights,
and all because
You taught me the secrets

of receiving joy
from *within*!
O Lord,
You heal the brokenhearted
(which I was),
and You bind up the wounds
of the damaged soul
(which I was).
I am once again
clear-eyed and laughing.
My joy is restored,
and I am a completely
new person!
Forever I will thank You.

My dear one,
I have much MORE
to give you. I spread out
My hands to you
to show you even greater and more
wonderful exploits in My
kingdom. Your praises ring throughout
the universe and all the heavenly
kingdom rejoices at the victories you

employ in love. Angels surround you
to celebrate My love with you.
It is love that triumphs in eternity, for love
is the language of heaven, and
love is the language
that unites heaven and earth. Your heart
of thanksgiving is burned into Mine
with the holy fire of My Spirit.
Love has given you a name,
and your love has brought glory to the earth.
This is My will on earth as it is
in heaven.

Psalm 147:3, 5–6; Matthew 22:32; Luke 24:5; Jeremiah 30:17; 3 John 2; Psalm 144:15, 145:18–20; Jeremiah 31:3; Revelation 3:5; Psalm 145:16; John 1:51; Matthew 6:9–10

THE GIFT OF ANOINTING

Now He who establishes us with you in Christ and has anointed us is God, who also has sealed us and given us the Spirit in our hearts as a guarantee.

2 CORINTHIANS 1:21–22 NKJV

I send you because you and I
are bonded together in My Spirit.
You care as I have shown you I care;
your arms are now *My* arms,
embracing the neglected, the wounded,
the loathsome, and the lost.
Your smile is now My smile,
enveloping the depressed and the hostile
atmosphere you move in. Your hands are now
My hands helping the weak and helpless;
your voice is now My voice
bringing hope to the cowardly and dying.
You are like a sweet perfume to a world
that has made its bed in garbage heaps.

You are a carrier of blessed light
to those who are without sight.
You carry with you the healing oil of
compassion; your ears are not deaf
to the cries of misery and loss;
you are unafraid of the malicious foe.

Because you and I are sealed by My Spirit,
no distance is too great for you to travel,
no river too raging, no terrain too ragged
as you climb the crags and search the pits
for those who have lost their souls while trying
to gain the world.
Brace up your heart, My beloved one;
set your face like a flint and listen
for the children crying, the hungry souls clamoring
for food, the rejected and despised weeping
for love. Do you feel the plight of those
crushed in spirit?
Go into all the world. *Go.*

---

2 Corinthians 2:15; Isaiah 12:2; Matthew 9:29; 17:20;
John 14:15–21; John 15:4–5; Luke 9:1–6; Matthew 28:18–20

Come Away With Me

My lover spoke and said to me,
"Arise, my darling, my beautiful one,
and come [away] with me."

Song of Songs 2:10 NIV

Beauty of days
    pulsing, throbbing,
    eager to fly higher,
to wear the garb
of fearlessness,
    to strip the glue
    from your toes,
kick the mud from your feet,
    lift up the hands that hang down,
jostle the clouds,
kiss the stars. Now is the time to
    take the gifts I offer you.
A thin gauze of underdeveloped faith
will never form a hero's armor,
    and now Majestic fingers
have woven a new coat for you.

Streaks of light dance from its sleeves;
gems and precious stones cast beams of light
from the lapel, and sparks fly from its pocket
carrying ignited answered prayers.
Rise up.
Rise up, I say!
Put on the magnificent
and come with Me!

Take more of My love and come.
I bless all your body, mind,
and soul with talents laced with mercy,
for I understand the journey,
which has taken you far.
You've traveled the ideas
and philosophies of great men and women;
you have searched and learned,
and asked many questions.
Every step you have taken
I have walked alongside you,
loving you, calling you,
wanting you.
And when your foot slipped,
it was I who caught you.

When the perverse leopard by the road
tried to kill you,
it was I who saved you.
We have barely begun,
you and I. Love Me with all your heart,
soul, and strength, and see
the best is yet to come.

Ephesians 6:10–11; Psalm 119:2; Isaiah 55:3;
Lamentations 3:22–23; Deuteronomy 6:5